Black Labor Migration in Caribbean Guatemala, 1882–1923

WORKING IN THE AMERICAS

UNIVERSITY PRESS OF FLORIDA

Florida A&M University, Tallahassee
Florida Atlantic University, Boca Raton
Florida Gulf Coast University, Ft. Myers
Florida International University, Miami
Florida State University, Tallahassee
New College of Florida, Sarasota
University of Central Florida, Orlando
University of Florida, Gainesville
University of North Florida, Jacksonville
University of South Florida, Tampa
University of West Florida, Pensacola

WORKING IN THE AMERICAS

Working in the Americas is devoted to publishing important works in labor history and working-class studies in the Americas. This series seeks work that uses both traditional as well as innovative, interdisciplinary, or transnational approaches. Its focus is the Americas and the lives of its workers.

Florida's Working Class Past: Current Perspectives on Labor, Race, and Gender from Spanish Florida to the New Immigration, edited by Robert Cassanello and Melanie Shell-Weiss (2008)

The New Economy and the Modern South, by Michael Dennis (2008)

Film Noir, American Workers, and Post-War Hollywood, by Dennis Broe (2009)

Americanization in the States: Immigrant Social Welfare Policy, Citizenship, and National Identity in the United States, 1908–1929, by Christina A. Ziegler-McPherson (2009)

Black Labor Migration in Caribbean Guatemala, 1882–1923, by Frederick Douglass Opie (2009)

Black Labor Migration in Caribbean Guatemala, 1882–1923

FREDERICK DOUGLASS OPIE

Foreword by Richard Greenwald and
Timothy J. Minchin, Series Editors

University Press of Florida
Gainesville/Tallahassee/Tampa/Boca Raton
Pensacola/Orlando/Miami/Jacksonville/Ft. Myers/Sarasota

Library of Congress Cataloging-in-Publication Data
Opie, Frederick Douglass.
Black labor migration in Caribbean Guatemala, 1882-1923 / Frederick Douglass
Opie ; foreword by Richard Greenwald and Timothy J. Minchin.
p. cm. — (Working in the Americas)
Includes bibliographical references and index.
ISBN 978-0-8130-3371-6 (alk. paper)
1. Alien labor—Guatemala—History. 2. African Americans—Guatemala—History.
3. Caribbean Area—Race relations—History. I. Title.
HD8146.O65 2009
331.6′20899607281—dc22
2009001966

The University Press of Florida is the scholarly publishing agency for the State
University System of Florida, comprising Florida A&M University, Florida At-
lantic University, Florida Gulf Coast University, Florida International University,
Florida State University, New College of Florida, University of Central Florida,
University of Florida, University of North Florida, University of South Florida,
and University of West Florida.

University Press of Florida
15 Northwest 15th Street
Gainesville, FL 32611-2079
http://www.upf.com

All photographs are from the United Fruit Company Photograph Collection,
Baker Library Historical Collection, Harvard University.

In Loving Memory of my father, Fred Opie Jr., who died of cancer just a month before this book was accepted for publication. Dad, I remember the overtime you worked at Sing Sing Prison to give me opportunities that you never had as a child. You taught me lessons about being disciplined as I worked for "Opie and Sons" janitorial services. Now I remember how I developed the discipline and work ethic necessary to finish this book. Dad, I remember that you were very well read and a gifted historian and archivist. This book in many ways is a reflection of your influence on my very eclectic historical curiosity. So I dedicate this book to you, Dad, the headman in the family—a real giver and a well-read Renaissance man. Finally, the book is dedicated to my wife Tina, who read and edited drafts of this book over many years.

Contents

Illustrations

Foreword

Until recently, most history was written within a national framework. But an increasing number of scholars are now eschewing this approach. In the last decade or so, increasingly sophisticated work has appeared that has documented the movement of both people and ideas across national boundaries. As its title indicates, Frederick Douglass Opie's study of African American and West Indians migrants in Guatemala is very much a transnational account. It brings to life a group of workers who have been neglected by scholars, and shows that they were "an important part of the larger history of the Atlantic world." It is a suitable and welcome addition to Working in the Americas, a series dedicated to exploring labor history and working-class life across the entire Americas.

As early as the 1850s, small numbers of American slaves fled to Guatemala, where they hoped to start afresh. These numbers really picked up after the abolishment of slavery and in the 1880s, however, after the Guatemalan government signed contracts with foreign companies to build an extensive railroad system. Faced with labor shortages, the railroads turned to black migrants from the West Indies and the United States to fill their worst-paying jobs (white-collar jobs were monopolized by whites). Although relatively small in number, these workers played an important role in building Guatemala's railroad system. The railroads facilitated the export of bananas and coffee, vital commodities to the economy of the Central American republic.

While conditions on the railroads were harsh, Opie explains that railroad work was nevertheless an attractive alternative to sharecropping or gang labor. It also provided an escape from the harsh Jim Crow laws that were coming into force across the American South. Seeking to escape poverty and discrimination, the black migrants found new problems in Guatemala, where they were "systematically taken advantage of by the labor agents, company supervisors, and Guatemalan officials."

Opie provides detailed portraits of many of the individuals who migrated to Guatemala and argues that they were often familiar with radical labor movements. Many migrated from New Orleans, where workers were particularly well organized in the late nineteenth century. Advancing a "revisionist interpretation," Opie stresses the agency of the African American laborers and shows how they resisted exploitation and played an important role in revolutionary movements in the late nineteenth and early twentieth centuries. In 1898, for example, black railroad workers participated in a failed strike. While detailing the conflicts that arose between black and Ladino workers, Opie also shows how the two groups banded together during subsequent strikes between 1909 and 1919. In addition, they actively participated in the 1920 revolution that removed the autocratic Estrada Cabrera from office.

This cooperation subsequently broke down, however, as fears of socialism led to foreign-born workers being treated with increased suspicion. Blacks and Ladinos now organized separately. In a final chapter, Opie analyzes the impact in Guatemala of Marcus Garvey's ideas, showing that black workers there used Garveyism "as a tool with which to organize and express solidarity." Garvey's United Negro Improvement Association also proved to be important in increasing the self-worth of black workers and in encouraging black business ownership.

Overall, Professor Opie's book succeeds in bringing a little-known story to light. Notwithstanding the hardships that the migrants faced, in the final analysis, Opie suggests, their move to Guatemala may have been worth it. "Despite its violent and corrupt government officials," he writes, "Guatemala proved to be an easier place for a black immigrant to become a property or business owner than the Jim Crow South or the British colonial West Indies." Black workers in Guatemala, he argues, also inspired subsequent labor activism and had an impact on the country's culture and politics that is still evident today.

Timothy J. Minchin
Richard Greenwald

Acknowledgments

Special thanks are due to several scholars who graciously read drafts of chapters of this project and provided valuable suggestions for improving the book; these include Dan North, George Reid Andrews, Delmar Ross, Michael Hanchard, Marc McLeod, and Franklin W. Knight.

I also want to thank the many librarians who made my job as a historian possible: Trevor Dawes, formerly of Columbia University Library; the Marist College librarians who handled my interlibrary loan requests; and the staff of the Hemeroteca de la Biblioteca Nacional de Guatemala, Guatemala City. Special thanks are also in order for the archivists at the National Archives in Washington, D.C., and at Archive II in College Park, Maryland; to the staff of the Archival General de Centro América in Guatemala City; and to the staff of the Baker Library at Harvard University.

Introduction

In 1884, steamships loaded with laborers from the U.S. ports of Mobile, Galveston, and New Orleans, and from the West Indies, began to arrive at the Caribbean port of Puerto Barrios, in Izabal, Guatemala. U.S. contractors had begun hiring black and Latin American workers to lay track throughout the Central American republic in the early 1880s, and black workers used the steamships to get to the railroad camps.[1] Many migrants who set sail for Guatemala were seeking to earn enough money to purchase property and improve their lives. Whether or not they managed to do so depended to a certain extent on the nature of their relationships with their employers as well as with the Guatemalan nationals they encountered.

This book focuses on black labor migration to Guatemala in the late nineteenth and early twentieth centuries, with particular attention to the experiences of black immigrants and their relations with Guatemalans and other Latin Americans. The earliest black workers came to Guatemala as contract laborers for railroad construction projects. The majority of them worked for what became the International Railroad of Central America (IRCA), and later for the United Fruit Company (UFCO) of Boston. Upon the completion of the lowland railroad projects in 1908, some men stayed on as employees of IRCA, while others took jobs with UFCO or worked in the capital city, in the interior of Guatemala. Starting in 1914, company officials on the Caribbean coast began hiring Guatemalan nationals to replace the migrant laborers. Thereafter, migrants increasingly became farmers or entrepreneurs and relocated to other parts of the Americas.

Prior to the Great Depression, foreign-born workers of African descent composed the largest segment of the Caribbean coast workforce in Guatemala. Between 1893 and 1918, they organized numerous labor movements in tandem with Guatemalan nationals. Unpaid back wages and intolerable working conditions on the coast proved decisive in prompting workers to strike and unionize. At that time, banana exporters depended on the Northern Railroad to ship bananas to the Caribbean coast for export. When railroad workers decided to strike, their goal was to shut down the railway lines that ran through the banana plantations all the way to the dock at Puerto Barrios.[2]

Turn-of-the-century Guatemala offered migrant workers opportunities, but it was nonetheless a dangerous and difficult place to make one's fortune.

U.S. State Department records point to a pattern of Guatemalan officials' carrying out violent anti-immigrant attacks against foreign laborers. Migrants of all nationalities suffered unprovoked thrashings at the hands of officials who used swords, rifle butts, and pistols to beat them into bloody submission. Rural officials arrested workers, particularly black migrants, without probable cause and then forced them to perform prison labor without trial or compensation. Black American prisoners in Guatemala spent years in jail cells without trial. Departmental governors acted as the military dictators of their departments. Judges and other officials were "merely puppets who eagerly appl[ied] the good law of the land to vicious purposes," as the governor directed them to do.[3] Departmental officials carried out acts of brutality without fear of reprimand because President Estrada Cabrera (1898–1920) usually protected them from charges of excessive use of force. The president himself carried on a reign of terror at the national level.[4] Conflict between laborers and officials in Guatemala arose because elites held in contempt workers in general, and black foreign workers especially. Caribbean coast workers engaged in a constant struggle for survival against their employers and Guatemalan officials.

Studies of Caribbean coast laborers are scarce to nonexistent, but where these workers are represented in the historical record, they tend to be depicted as passive pawns of their employers and victims of state repression during the repressive dictatorship of President Estrada Cabrera. This book advances a revisionist interpretation, arguing that workers of African descent have played an important role in Guatemala's history since the 1880s when liberal elites first revamped the republic's economic development and modernization plan. Indeed, the history of black labor in lowland Guatemala is an important part of the larger history of the Atlantic World.[5] Dockworkers and railroad employees in particular had considerable influence on national events due to the central role of coffee and banana exports in the Guatemalan economy. Caribbean coast workers in Guatemala proved to be important political allies during revolutionary movements against José María Reyna Barrios in 1897 and Manuel José Estrada Cabrera in 1920, and their activism nearly toppled the government a third time in 1923.[6] Even under the repressive Estrada Cabrera regime, laborers in Guatemala mobilized and conducted impromptu strikes.[7]

In revisiting and rewriting the history of black workers in Guatemala, this book concentrates on the Guatemalan departments of Izabal and Zacapa, where two Caribbean coast African diaspora communities developed with multiple black identities, including black Americans, black West Indians of various national identities, and Garifuna, or "black Caribs," as they were once known.

Traditionally, scholars working on Central America have chosen to focus on the experiences of West Indian migrants. The large number of workers and the long-term influence of West Indians in the region make studies of their migration invaluable.[8] This book, however, seeks to broaden our understanding of race relations in the circum-Caribbean and Guatemala.[9]

Class, gender, and ideology were far more important than skin pigmentation alone in shaping race relations in Guatemala. On the Caribbean coast, black American men had cordial relations with Guatemalan women and regular conflicts with Guatemalan men. In the same locale, however, West Indian men had a history of bad relations with Guatemalan men and women. In general, Caribbean coast race relations were steeped in economic issues and nationalistic ideology, which were closely intertwined. For instance, poorly paid Guatemalan soldiers regularly expressed their contempt for black foreign nationals because U.S.- and British-operated enterprises preferred hiring English-speaking blue-collar workers for better-than-average-paying jobs. Local-level Guatemalan officials harassed black foreign nationals, therefore, because they thought of British subjects and Americans as English speakers who monopolized the plum jobs on the Caribbean coast. Corrupt local officials regularly attempted to extort money and labor from black workers and black entrepreneurs. Conflict between black laborers and Guatemalan workers most often happened on paydays, when workers with money to spend frequented bars, casinos, and makeshift dice games. In these spaces, workers who lost money to others or who were otherwise offended sought to right perceived wrongs with revolvers, knives, and machetes. After such altercations, the Guatemalan state came to the aid of its nationals, using police brutality to subdue black suspects. In addition, the state arbitrarily beat and jailed black foreign nationals and forced them to perform prison labor. In contrast to their treatment of working-class blacks, state officials used far more restraint in their interactions with upper-class white foreigners, especially UFCO and IRCA managers. Guatemalan soldiers showed deference toward UFCO and IRCA's white elites because of the political support they had from the U.S. and U.K. governments.

Although the history of black migration to Guatemala is often interpreted through the lens of middle- and upper-class observers, a careful examination of the public and private letters of migrants, journalists, government officials, and employers provides important insights into the agency of a multiethnic workforce during the autocratic rule of Estrada Cabrera. These sources tell us that, with various degrees of success and failure, workers regularly engaged in strikes and organized trade unions. In addition, workers actively participated in the 1920 revolution that removed Estrada Cabrera from office. It is challenging to write the history of workers whose "departures were frequent and destinations rarely final," as one historian put it.[10] In addition, the workers in this story left few written sources about their union activities and labor conflicts with their employers. The story told in this volume necessarily contains gaps where the historical record is not forthcoming with details: in some cases, it's impossible to know whether a group of striking workers was made up of Latin Americans (or, again, mestizos) alone or whether it also contained Jamaicans, black Americans, or Garifuna. As a rule, individual laborers appear in the records only briefly, leaving no clue as to what happened to them in their later lives. And solid figures regarding the number of laborers of different ethnicities who were employed on the Caribbean coast at different times are equally impossible to obtain. As the historian Bradford Burns has stated, however, a "paucity of conventional documentation complicates but should not impede the search for popular preferences."[11] We must do what we can with the records that exist.

Sources consulted for this project include travel accounts, private manuscript collections, novels, and government archival holdings. Research in U.S., Guatemalan, and British archives yielded letters and affidavits written or dictated by foreign workers. Extensive use of Guatemalan newspapers provided valuable insights into local, national, and international political developments directly and indirectly related to workers. British records show that West Indians participated in railroad, dock, and plantation strikes on the Caribbean coast. Most of the Americans in Guatemala worked on the railroads that stretched across the nation, with very few working on UFCO plantations.

Evidence of the actual size of the railroad and banana workforce and the ethnicity of the workers appears sporadically in the documentary record and therefore is not complete enough to draw any empirical conclusions. What we do have are snapshots from several different sources, including Guatemalan periodicals and diplomatic records. Between 1884 and 1894, for example, Guatemalan newspapers and Guatemalan and U.S. officials reported the arrival of workers in groups of as few as 19 and as many as 112 men on individual steamships. At times these reports described the ethnicity of the men.[12] Although it is unclear how many returned to the United States and the West Indies, we can estimate that about 2,500 to 5,000 black Americans and another 15,000 to 20,000 black West Indians migrated to the Caribbean coast of Guatemala between 1863 and 1923.[13] We also have evidence from a U.S. consulate report stating that approximately 10,000 passengers entered Guatemala in 1914. Of these, 2,327 were Guatemalans, 4,607 were "foreign whites," and 3,380 were "foreign negroes" (among them West Indians of all stripes and black Americans).[14] Some of the earliest black migrants arrived as consigned laborers to railroad camps in Guatemala directly from New Orleans, other southern ports, and West Indian ports. Others arrived in Guatemala indirectly from the Panama Canal Zone and other locations of foreign investment in Nicaragua, Honduras, Belize, El Salvador, Costa Rica, and Mexico.[15]

Overview

To understand the reception of black immigrant laborers in Guatemala in the late nineteenth and early twentieth centuries, it is necessary to first consider the history of attitudes toward black workers in Guatemala. Chapter 1 therefore begins with this history, outlining the long tradition of prejudice against people of African descent in the country.[16] It then delves into the history of railroad construction and economic development in Guatemala, explaining why the construction project came to be run by foreign-owned companies and why it required black laborers to be imported from the United States and the Caribbean. By then shifting to the laborers' perspective, I also consider what drew them to migrate to Guatemala for work and how they were recruited. Foreign nationals from around the world often arrived in Puerto Barrios, Guatemala, after extensive travel and work experiences on rail networks across the southern United States, Guatemala, and other parts of the Americas stretching from Mexico to Brazil. Black workers performed similar railroad work in Costa Rica, Panama, and other parts of Latin America, but eventually came to dominate jobs also in the banana and sugar industries in the circum-Caribbean.[17]

Turning to the subject of work conditions and labor mobilization, in chapter 2 I look at conditions on the Caribbean coast and consider how the ethnically diverse coastal migrant workers were exploited by labor agents and their corporate employers, with the assistance of hostile local Guatemalan officials. The chapter argues that in Guatemala, foreign workers of the 1880s and 1890s shared a common experience of abuse at the hands of employers and military authorities. It also looks at some early evidence of workers' resistance to this poor treatment: in the early 1880s, workers struggled together against employers and the state for back wages during depressions and to improve their situation overall. In 1897, during a revolutionary period, workers took up arms against the Guatemalan state, displaying a cross-race solidarity that is explored further in later chapters.

The following two chapters focus on relationships among coastal workers, beginning in chapter 3 with a discussion of interethnic conflict among workers. This chapter argues that a shift in the composition of the coastal workforce to include more Latin Americans, combined with strengthening anti-immigrant sentiment among Guatemalans and the passage of unfavorable anti-immigrant legislation, worked to exacerbate conflict among Latin American and black workers. At the same time, the chapter also points to the fact that alcohol and gambling, rather than racist or nationalistic sentiments, proved the most important factors in causing violent conflict and divisions among Caribbean coast workers.[18] Chapter 4 then argues that despite their differences, black and Latin American workers from diverse backgrounds managed to unite against their racist bosses in order to agitate for better work conditions. The chapter looks at a series of strikes from the period 1909–19 in detail, showing how workers banded together across ethnic and national lines in a united effort to improve the quality of their lives.[19] This chapter challenges the depiction of the coastal workforce, often found in scholarly works, as hopelessly divided along ethnic and cultural lines, and as completely passive in the face of company domination.

Still, the cooperation described in chapter 4 was relatively fleeting. By 1918, the tensions between Guatemalan nationals and black immigrants in the labor force largely prevented the cooperation that had characterized the labor mobilization of the decade before. The nationalistic goals of organized Guatemalan laborers had helped to create public laws and company policies that ended the competition that nationals faced from foreign workers for skilled and unskilled Caribbean coast jobs. Incidents of anti-immigrant acts and nationalism on the Caribbean coast of Guatemala had picked up steam following the outbreak of the Mexican Revolution in 1910, and Central American officials, fearing the spread of Bolshevism to Guatemalan laborers, were especially hard on foreigners coming from Mexico.

Chapters 5 and 6 discuss the ways in which Latin American and black laborers, rather than fight together for their rights as workers, mobilized separately in the years following the First World War. Latin American workers on the Caribbean coast joined in and contributed to the 1920 overthrow of President Estrada Cabrera, but their radicalism was increasingly nationalist, anti-imperialist, and racist, pitting them against the company and its North American employees as well as against the black, English-speaking workers whose jobs they envied. Chapter 5 explores this history and places the labor militancy of Guatemalan nationals of the early 1920s in the context of numerous global and regional radical movements. In that decade, the Russian Revolution fueled labor politics throughout the Western world, including the Americas. Unionized Guatemalan railroad workers established correspondence with Mexican railroad unions. The 1920s saw the establishment of socialist labor organizations and branches of the Communist Party in Mexico and Central America.[20] Radicals from El Salvador and Honduras played important roles in organizing Caribbean coast workers, as was evident during a 1923 labor strike against United Fruit Company managers.[21]

In this same period, black Caribbean coast workers were organizing under the influence of Garveyism; this subject is investigated in chapter 6. Starting in the 1920s, Marcus Garvey's followers founded local branches of the Universal Negro Improvement Association (UNIA) in the United States, Jamaica, and Central America. The UNIA played an important role in uniting black migrant workers from various cultures and societies together, fostering solidarity and confidence within an organizational infrastructure that enabled them to mobilize against their employers in ways that Garvey himself might have discouraged.[22]

The book concludes by considering the significance of the history of black migrant laborers in Guatemala and their place in the coastal workforce. For the freedmen who started immigrating as early as 1853, travel to Guatemala represented an escape from the white racist–controlled Jim Crow U.S. South and the French and British colonial Caribbean. Labor recruiters spread the word that Guatemala was "the next Booming Country," where "White and Colored Laborers" could work for the railroad, save enough money to buy land, and become rich off of the turn-of-the-century frenzy for cultivating and selling bananas on the international market. As we shall see, for some, immigration to Guatemala provided an opportunity to purchase property and pursue entrepreneurial ambitions that would have been hard to achieve in the economically depressed and politically repressive regions the immigrants came from. But the effect of immigration on the history of Guatemala was even more profound, as migrant and Latin American laborers' militancy, though largely unsuccessful, paved the way for the struggles of later workers and permanently transformed the culture of Caribbean Guatemala.

1

Historical Context

Race and Labor in Guatemala

Before the 1990s, research on Guatemalan history commonly overlooked the contributions of people of African descent to the development of the railroad and banana industries. Despite the integral role of black laborers in these vital industries, historians doing work on Guatemala have given preference to studies of the relations between the indigenous and the Spanish, or between indigenous people and mestizos. Until recently, this trend in scholarship only stressed relations between the Africans and the Spanish within a slavery and servitude framework, overlooking relations between Indians and Africans. Starting in the 1990s, several scholars began providing an overdue revision of this neglect of people of African descent.[1] This chapter builds on their work, highlighting the long history of the African presence in Guatemala and providing a context for understanding relations between black migrant laborers and Guatemalan nationals on the Caribbean coast. It begins with an overview of Spanish attitudes toward blacks and mulattoes in the colonial period, before moving on to discuss how Guatemalan politics and economic priorities in the national period created a need for foreign involvement in railroad development, as well as foreign laborers to build the railroads. Subsequent sections of the chapter discuss how black laborers from Jamaica and the United States were recruited, as well as the tradition of labor radicalism that some Southern black workers brought to Guatemala with them.

The Colonial Period

We now know that from their first arrival in the Americas, the Spaniards viewed African slaves as essential to the conquest of the region that is now Guatemala. By the early 1540s, enslaved Africans entered Guatemala through a Caribbean coast port in Honduras. More slaves entered Guatemala during the sixteenth century on the whole than surviving records might indicate.

Europeans imported slaves indirectly from Mexico, Panama, Colombia, and the far reaches of colonial Guatemala. For two and half centuries, those who entered Guatemala did so under royal license or as contraband trade. By the end of the sixteenth century, Afro-Guatemalan populations had developed in different pockets of colonial Guatemala. Spaniards depended on enslaved African laborers on the few sugar plantations in the region. Over 1,100 people of African descent lived in the capital of Guatemala in the 1590s. Populations of mulattos of both Indian and African descent of a similar size could be found in regions outside the capital.

As the indigenous population recovered from the death and destruction of the Spanish conquest, Spaniards imported very few enslaved Africans into Guatemala between 1640 and the end of the seventeenth century.[2] Because of this, and due to miscegenation between slaves and free people, the presence of African slaves in Guatemala declined. In fact, one hundred years after their importation, African communities had become mulatto communities, and had replaced indigenous communities on the Pacific coast. Africans worked in the mining, sugar, indigo, and textile industries. Prior to the seventeenth century, colonial officials had sought to use African slaves to perform harsh jobs deemed too difficult for Indians. Starting in the seventeenth century, people of African descent served as members of the colonial militia, mustering out to protect the colony from foreign enemies.[3]

Unlike the West Indian population, the population of males of African descent in Guatemala never came close to replacing the indigenous population as the Spanish colonists' primary source of labor. Still, from the late seventeenth century to the early eighteenth century, people of African descent "neither disappeared quickly or naturally," as historian Paul Lokken put it.[4] Close contact in both urban and rural settings led to miscegenation involving Iberians, Africans, and Indians. This long-term pattern lightened the complexion of Afro-Guatemalans between the mid-seventeenth century and the early nineteenth century. Enslaved African men showed a strong proclivity toward procreating with Indian or mixed-race women. Less often, enslaved African women procreated with Spaniards. A study by Christopher Lutz and Matthew Restall explains: "Due to the 'law of the womb,' whereby children fathered by slaves were themselves born slaves only if their mothers were enslaved, a large slave and free population of African descent emerged. . . . These children of mixed descent were almost always identified as being mulatto . . . whether their second parent was Maya or Spaniard."[5]

How were people of African descent viewed in Guatemalan society? During the sixteenth century, Spaniards viewed Africans born in the Americas as possessing greater worth than those born in Africa. Likewise, Spaniards viewed those mulattos immersed in Iberian culture with greater esteem than unacculturated mixed-raced groups. Spaniards valued the skills and language fluency of mulattos in addition to their fairer skin. Culturally, Spaniards also viewed male Africans as more valuable workers than females, which created gender imbalances in the colony. Because slaves were very costly, the Spaniards imported them in limited numbers and valued their labor more than that of the Indians. Untrained African slaves were considered to be investments. Once taught a valued skill, they could be sold within the colony for a profit. Within the colonial hierarchy, Spaniards considered Africans, who often worked as supervisors, to be a people of higher status than Indians because Africans served as valuable go-betweens in relationships involving Spanish employers and their indigenous employees. Similarly, in the colonial economy, Spanish employers often pressured their African managers and overseers to physically compel Indian subordinates to produce more under the *repartimiento* system, which utilized a forced rotational labor draft that relocated Indian laborers from their home communities for two to four months at a time.[6]

Although the Spanish relied upon the skills of Africans, they were troubled by the growing numbers of Africans and mulattos in Guatemala. As in other parts of the Americas, communities of escaped slaves strengthened and increased in size in Guatemala. Spanish authorities tried to control enslaved Africans and runaways by using black militiamen, but their efforts were often futile. Over time, the prices of slaves decreased as Europeans purchased more of them, and Africans began to outnumber Europeans. With the support of Spanish patrons who depended on the productive skills of trained slaves for their livelihood, Guatemala's population of people of African descent freely disregarded the law. At times, gangs of African slaves, armed and mounted on horseback, wandered at will. These roustabouts showed little fear of Spanish authorities and treated other Europeans with insolence. Authorities resorted to restraining threatening blacks and mulattos in an effort to teach them to respect the colonial social hierarchy. The ratio of Africans and mulattos to Europeans made enforcement difficult however. News of an alleged conspiracy of blacks and mulattos involving twenty-nine men and four women in Mexico City in 1612 also increased Europeans' fear of blacks in Guatemala. As a result, Spanish citizens pressured town councils to prohibit the importation of Africans.[7]

The 1648 travel account of Thomas Gage provides an eyewitness view with which to interpret how Europeans perceived people of African descent during the colonial period. Gage visited indigo plantations and cattle haciendas on the southern coast of Guatemala. He also traversed the mountain region near the Caribbean coast, where people of African descent had established Maroon communities in which runaways lived like pirates. These communities, nestled in the rugged terrain, were known for the rebellious attitude of their residents. Elites living in nearby regions expressed a constant fear of desperate, machete-wielding enslaved Africans, and were terrified by the idea of Maroon communities of two to three hundred armed runaways. Gage surmised that "all the power of Guatemala, nay all that country about (having often attempted it), is not able to bring [the Maroons] under subjection."[8]

Armed with "bows and arrows," the Maroons regularly attacked and plundered Spanish and Indian villages in the coastal region. Maroons also ambushed caravans that passed through territories under their control. Because these caravans were usually transporting goods, the ambushes could provide the Maroons with "wine, iron, clothing and weapons." The Spanish were particularly irked by the autonomous Maroons because their escapes from servitude caused those in captivity to "rejoice with them" about their free status and seeming invincibility before slaveholders and state authorities. The Maroons' example encouraged many enslaved Africans to escape and join one of the several hundred Maroon communities that existed during the colonial period.[9]

Newly arriving slaves from Africa were a critical source for Maroon recruitment. After 1630, the number of new arrivals decreased drastically. This demographic change stifled the continued growth of large-scale Maroon communities over the intervening years, similarly to other parts of the Americas.[10] Slavery was abolished in Guatemala the Kingdom in 1824. Even before the abolition of slavery, blacks in Guatemala, outside of the Garifuna of the town of Livingston, were disappearing. This was due to declining imports after 1630 and miscegenation with largely Mayan and mestizo mates. Close contact in both urban and rural settings led to miscegenation involving black men and brown women. This long-term pattern lightened the complexion of Afro-Guatemalans between the late colonial and early national periods. Due to racism and classism, Central American societies generally rejected their black populations and treated them poorly.[11] In addition, the constant threat of armed revolution at the turn of the century contributed to the mistreatment of English-speaking, working-class black immigrants in the Caribbean region of Central America, where railroads were being built. Central American authorities in general were "very suspicious of all foreigners, especially those who spoke English," reported a U.S. diplomat in Honduras in 1910.[12] This is because those who were wealthy enough to bankroll the military overthrow of a government often hired

English-speaking foreign mercenaries, like General Lee Christmas, to do their bidding. Though Christmas was white, he spoke English, and so did the black workers who immigrated to work on the railroads in Honduras, Guatemala, and other parts of the region in the national period.[13]

Railroad Construction and Politics in the National Period

In 1877, President Justo Rufino Barrios (1873–85) launched the construction of a modern transportation system in Guatemala. The Guatemalan railway system was to have four principal lines: the Central Railroad, the Western Railroad, the Ocós Railroad, and the Northern Railroad. One important purpose of the state-owned system would be to enable coffee growers in the several mountainous highland departments to ship coffee, via the Northern Railroad, to Puerto Barrios, where a modern port was to be built on the Caribbean coast. This would allow the growers to circumvent the U.S.-operated Pacific Mail Steamship Company, which monopolized railway transportation and shipping from Guatemala's only deep-water ocean port, at San José on the Pacific coast. Creating new rail lines and a new Caribbean port promised to help Guatemalan coffee growers become more competitive, boosting exports and improving the national economy.[14]

The government signed contracts with foreign companies to build the railroads. The Northern was to be constructed by Tully Cornick Jr. and Shea Cornick of Knoxville, Tennessee, and by J. H. Lyman and J. B. Gordon of New York. Contract provisions required the government to "provide from three to five thousand laborers as needed," according to historian Delmar Ross.[15] For a time, the Guatemalan state succeeded in using coffee proceeds to pay for the construction of the railroad—until Brazil entered the international coffee market, driving prices down and causing financial difficulties that eventually stalled railroad construction, which came to a complete halt in April 1885 with the death of Rufino Barrios. The Guatemalan government, under heavy foreign debt obligations (particularly to England), had to either retire the English debt or grant North American investors favorable concessions.[16] It decided on the latter course and began constructing a relationship with North American investors who had the capital and the technical know-how to construct a railroad. In 1904, Henry F. W. Nanne, the general manager of Minor C. Keith's Costa Rican Railway, negotiated a final contract with the state to complete the Northern Line. Keith would gain the construction and operating rights for the Guatemalan Northern Railroad and would eventually come to monopolize the entire Guatemalan railway system.[17] It would be private Guatemalan entrepreneurs and (mostly foreign) railroad investors, then, and not the government, that launched banana cultivation and exports on the Caribbean coast. Under the new arrangement, the Guatemalan government would own the railroad tracks, but Keith's company would lease and manage them, as well as the labor force.[18]

In 1892, President Manuel Lisandro Barillas (1885–91) arranged for one of Guatemala's few peaceful presidential transitions with the democratic election of José María Reyna Barrios (1892–97), a nephew of Justo Rufino Barrios. On March 15, 1892, Democratic Party candidate Reyna Barrios took possession of the presidency by popular election, defeating Liberal Party candidate Lorenzo Montúfar and Conservative candidates General Miguel Enríquez and José Llerena. At the time, Guatemala had two political groups: Liberals and Conservatives. Central American Liberals came from the same wealthy land and elitist class as their Conservative opponents rather than from the "aspiring middle classes or petty bourgeoisie" that was historically active during revolutions. In Guatemala, however, the Liberal faction was consistently hostile to old-money merchants and landowners, and it included a substantial number of Hispanics of more modest social origins. In addition, Guatemalan Liberals tended to include elite yet less politically influential coffee producers from departments like Alta Verapaz in northwest Guatemala.[19] The conflict between the two parties was one of old versus new money. As historians Lowell Gudmundson and Héctor Lindo-Fuentes argue, "New money and blood might dispute old money and quasi-nobility, but money and personal political dominance remained the basic pattern and goal."[20] The contempt that Liberals and Conservatives expressed toward one another was equaled only by that which they directed toward peasants and laborers. According to Gudmundson and Lindo-Fuentes, these groups did not exist politically in the minds of elite Liberals or Conservatives, "except as pawns in a game with other power contenders."[21] Guatemalan politics of the late nineteenth and early twentieth centuries were frequently characterized by violent presidential changes, the absence of democratic elections, and the participation of working-class groups in conflicts between the leadership of the Liberal and Conservative parties.

Both parties employed caudillo politics: politics in which a political boss used violence and fear to dominate government agencies and decisions. In the era from the 1880s to the 1920s, Liberal caudillos like Reyna Barrios disregarded the popular will and the democratically elected representatives in the National Assembly. Reyna's political platform championed the continuation of archaic compulsory labor laws that guaranteed the availability of unskilled laborers for public works projects. Perhaps the hallmark of his platform, however, was the continued modernization of the country's transportation infrastructure in order to increase revenues from banana and coffee exports. During his presidency, Reyna Barrios spent a great deal of the national treasury on transportation projects.[22]

Recruiting Labor

Until the turn of the twentieth century, the peasant Garifuna (or "Caribs" in early records) of Guatemala, Belize, and Honduras operated well-established subsistence economies and showed little interest in wage-labor jobs. The Garifuna were runaway slaves and other fugitives who created autonomous Maroon communities; they had relocated to Central America from the British colony of Saint Vincent in the West Indies in the late eighteenth century.[23] Not until the 1910s did they begin working as stevedores loading and unloading bananas on Caribbean coast docks, like those of Puerto Barrios. Guatemalans also refused to work on the Caribbean coast because it was infested with malaria. This meant that employers, from the mid-nineteenth century, had to recruit laborers from outside of Guatemala.[24] Both Conservative- and Liberal-controlled governments in Guatemala wished to promote white immigration and to discourage the importation of black migrants, believing that white immigrants could positively influence Guatemala's largely Mayan population. But until 1914, that desire competed with the country's need for black immigrants to fill Caribbean coast labor shortages during the construction of the railroad.

In the 1860s, the Guatemalan government had offered various types of aid and privileges to white immigrants willing to settle and cultivate regions of the Caribbean coast. The government's settlement program had offered the land adjacent to the Northern Railroad to one million white foreigners interested in raising families and farming cocoa, sugar, oranges, pines, nutmeg, and coffee. In an effort to recruit more workers and encourage the cultivation of bananas, which emerged as a profitable export for Guatemala in the mid-1880s, the state now promised 27-acre homesteads in the fertile Motagua River Valley in the Department of Izabal to American laborers who agreed to come to Guatemala to work on the railroad, stipulating that the homesteaders had to remain employed on the railroad for at least one year and then had to cultivate and live on their homestead for five years to obtain permanent title.[25] A presidential decree published in 1885 stated that the government's aim was to attract honest immigrants to promote large-scale banana cultivation in uninhabited backwater departments like Izabal and Zacapa.[26] The state also provided the homesteaders with subsidies to cultivate bananas, thus ensuring that the Northern Railroad would have the freight necessary to meet its operating costs.

In the 1880s, finding laborers was the colonists' biggest challenge. Local authorities coerced and monopolized the available Indian labor for their own ends. Before immigration restrictions were established in 1897, Guatemalan authorities permitted the importation of foreign laborers from the Americas, Europe, and Asia to alleviate labor demands.[27] In 1895, for example, the North American immigrants Byron Tunnel (a white man) and Sherman Taylor (a black man) came to Guatemala to fill a demand for farmhands on a 700-acre coffee farm called La Viña. The owner of the estate promised to supply Tunnel and his wife, Bella, with the necessary corn to start their own farm on the Caribbean coast. The Tunnels and other white North Americans found better opportunities in Guatemala than they did in the United States. Land was available, and, with some effort, farming provided a good income. Most white immigrants worked for only a few years before their employer assisted them in starting their own farms. The record indicates, however, that black hands at La Viña did not receive the same assistance.[28] In lowland frontier towns life for black farmhands was difficult and dangerous. If a tropical disease did not kill them, a lynch mob might.

Some black laborers also arrived as homesteaders themselves; indeed, the Guatemalan homestead offer was probably more attractive to black Americans than to whites: better homestead offers existed on the western frontier of the United States for white Americans, but according to historian Ross, black Americans, particularly former slaves, "as victims of racial discrimination often found it difficult to prove up and gain title to their homesteads in the United States."[29]

Many immigrants arrived in Guatemala after a stint working on the failed French canal project in Panama that had been undertaken between 1850 and 1880. Workers had migrated to Panama from various regions of the Americas, Europe, Africa, and Asia. Those from the West Indies represented the most important source of labor.[30] In the year 1882 alone, more than a thousand Jamaicans per month had migrated to Panama, Mexico, and Yucatán. Writing from Panama in November 1883, a British rear admiral named Lyons observed that "about 2,000 Europeans, for the most part French," were engaged on the canal project, along with 13,000 unskilled laborers, "chiefly Jamaica negroes and natives of Central America."[31] In February 1884, the *New York Times* reported, "between 15,000 and 20,000 Jamaica negroes are employed under the direction of the French engineers."[32] In all, about 50,000 West Indians migrated to Panama as laborers in the 1850s. Many of these laborers migrated several different times, spending time in one Latin American country, then another. They might be brought in to subdue malaria-infested swamp regions, but after their work was done, their employers would cut their wages, forcing them to migrate to another country, where they would again work to make a swamp region livable and arable. Many of the thousands of workers who migrated to Panama in search of work later left for jobs in other parts of Latin America.[33]

Recruiting foreign workers in the late nineteenth century was a complex process involving government officials from the host country, multinational corporations, labor recruiters, laborers, and government officials from the sending country. In a January 1896 letter to the Guatemalan minister of development, the superintendent of the Northern Railroad, F. García, explained, "The greatest difficulty with which I have to struggle in this work, is the lack of manual labor and the un-usefulness of the ones that they obtained." In the pursuit of suitable laborers, García sent labor recruiters to Nicaragua.[34] These recruiters apparently went to the West Indian community of Blue Fields on the Caribbean coast of Nicaragua, where in January 1896 they acquired "100 men of hot climate and accustomed to railroad work." The Guatemalan Ministry of Development paid the workers' transportation and docking fees in Guatemala, as well as their housing expenses. García had to negotiate with Nicaraguan president José Santos Zelaya in order to gain permission for the workers to travel back and forth between the two countries. In addition to federal officials, García called upon the assistance of local departmental authorities in recruiting workers.[35]

In the 1897 agreement between one contractor and the Guatemalan government, one of the stipulations was that foreign workers on the Northern Railroad project "will be considered [before the law] as Guatemalans in every aspect referred to thereby." The same article went on to say that foreigners would only "have the rights and measures of doing that which the laws of the Republic concede to Guatemalans, they cannot depend on having intervention from any [d]iplomatic agents." This last article was important, because it gave Guatemalan officials the latitude they needed to help multinational corporations meet their labor demands and thereby fulfill their government contracts.[36] In agreements signed after 1897, Guatemalan officials eliminated the obligation of the government to use its employees and resources to import foreign workers. Now multinational corporations were allowed the right to "freely import the foreign workers" that they needed, but the company had to bear the costs.[37] These concessions also gave companies the right to recruit the foreign workers of their choice, regardless of nationality, color, or class. Workers were drawn from the United States, Jamaica,

China, Italy, Germany, England, Ireland, France, El Salvador, Honduras, Nicaragua, and Mexico, and local Guatemalans were also pressed into service, by force on occasion.[38] But contractors established strong preferences over time for workers of particular ethnicities and nationalities for different jobs, effectively racializing various occupations. F. G. Williamson, general manager of the Guatemalan Railroad, wrote to the American foreign minister in Guatemala, Leslie Combs, that he preferred to hire "Jamaican negroes" as workers, since "whites . . . could not stand the climate and, anyhow, did not come here to work," while black Americans were "inferior in average intelligence to the Jamaican negroes."[39] In the early years of railroad construction, however, from 1884 to 1904 there were probably between 2,000 and 2,500 black American immigrants working in Guatemala. The first large boatload of West Indian workers (200 of them) did not arrive until 1893.[40] After the arrival of the United Fruit Company in 1901 the population of West Indians began to surpass the population of black Americans in Guatemala, and dominated the landscape of the banana enclaves and small towns near the provincial centers along the Northern Railroad. U.S. corporations contracted directly with British colonial authorities for the shipment of Jamaican workers, and sometimes they contracted directly with labor agents in Jamaica.[41] In Jamaica, the labor agents had emerged from a class of wealthy businessmen and smaller traders who had provided services to the French during the Panama canal project. Many of them had begun their careers in the trading of goods between Jamaica and different parts of Central America. Recruiting first started in urban towns and cities, such as Kingston, and then spread into rural villages, where it had a substantial economic impact.[42]

They Came from the West Indies

Due to a number of factors, a large supply of workers was available for emigration from the West Indies in the late nineteenth and early twentieth centuries. Beginning in 1867, British authorities passed several laws that called for the confiscation of lands with unpaid taxes, which effectively led to the dislocation of numerous small Jamaican farmers and squatters. Many of the dislocated individuals in Jamaica opted to pursue job opportunities in Central America.[43] The failure of small Jamaican farmers and the breakup of small peasant freeholds exacerbated rural proletarianization. To make matters worse, during the 1880s the European beet-sugar industry, with government encouragement and subsidies, substantially increased its output. The result was a sharp decline in the price of sugar between 1881 and 1896. Over time, European beet-sugar producers displaced Caribbean sugar exporters in the European market. Ultimately, the shift in the world sugar market devastated Jamaican sugar estates, along with the interrelated businesses and the workers they employed. Finally, as less-profitable Jamaican sugar estates went out of business, the demand for artisans and craftsmen in the sugar industry decreased. Many of these unemployed Jamaican workers abandoned the agricultural sector and moved into towns where they joined the growing ranks of the island's urban floating-labor reserve. This reserve labor was forced to remain mobile in order to respond to unstable market conditions.[44]

In short, the erosion of the Jamaican sugar industry made Jamaicans from sugar-producing regions geographically mobile. Thereafter, laborers ignored state-constructed impediments to their mobility and negotiated the sale of their labor to the country of their choice. Railroad contractors made use of newspapers and informal information networks to advertise the existence of jobs with competitive wages, food and lodging, and medical care in Central America. Moreover, many Jamaicans migrated to Cuba and Guatemala without the assistance of labor recruiters. According to Frederic J. Haskin, who investigated labor recruiting, less than two years after the start of the Panama canal construction, little labor recruiting was necessary in the West Indies: "Every ship that went back to Barbados or to Jamaica carried with it some who had made what they considered a sufficient fortune." Returnees came "with savings enough to set them up for life." Haskin continued: "This fired dozens from each of those same communities with the desire to go and do likewise. The result was that the canal employment lists were kept full by those who came on their own initiative."[45]

From Panama, many of these West Indian workers made their way to Guatemala. Again, sometimes companies sent labor recruiters to Panama to pay for their passage, and other times workers came at their own expense and initiative. In June 1893, *El Norte*, a Caribbean coast newspaper in Guatemala, reported on the arrival of workers on board the steamship *Engineer*, "proceeding from Panama: with 92 passengers for the railroad."[46] The new immigrants transformed the bordering departments of Izabal and Zacapa into a provincial African diaspora occupied by blacks of various nationalities.

They Came from the Southern United States

Similar to their West Indian colleagues, both white and black North Americans who migrated to Guatemala often arrived there after stints in other parts of Latin America. Most often, they departed the United States from the docks of New Orleans; Mobile, Alabama; or Galveston, Texas. In the late nineteenth and early twentieth century, workers came from Texas; Howard

County, Missouri; Ohio; California; the Carolinas; Kentucky; Americus and Atlanta, Georgia; Virginia; Louisiana; Meridian, Natchez, Aberdeen, and Komper County, Mississippi; and Montgomery and Jefferson County, Alabama.[47]

At the end of the nineteenth century, the populations of the cities of the U.S. South skyrocketed, as increasing numbers of both blacks and whites abandoned the plantations of the Black Belt for the greater opportunities available in the South's developing towns and cities. Employers in New Orleans used the tactic of dispatching labor agents to Southern port cities to acquire large numbers of replacement workers to defeat striking employees. Southern blacks also freely pursued construction and track crew jobs, in spite of the severity of the work and the sporadic compulsion labor recruiters used. They viewed wage labor in the railroad industry as an attractive alternative to gang labor, sharecropping, or plantation work. Railroads paid them higher cash wages than anything they might earn performing agricultural work. Historian Eric Arnesen found that "Black men seeking to supplement their families' income might take seasonal leave of the plantation in search of more remunerative employment, often returning home only at harvest time."[48] In New Orleans, railroad officials depended on a large reserve of itinerant laborers who journeyed to the Crescent City during the winter months in search of work. During sudden labor shortages, Southern railroad officials sent labor recruiters to local bars, poorhouses, and hobo encampments to secure workers. The numbers of the destitute in New Orleans became so large that officials there reestablished their workhouse facilities and restored the chain gang for the unemployed and homeless. Blacklisted striking workers in the coal mining industry of Jefferson County, Alabama, near Birmingham, often took to the road in the late nineteenth century in search of better opportunities. Thousands of workers relocated to cities like New Orleans in search of new jobs as employers imported replacement workers to break mining industry strikes.[49]

Both black and white migrants from the southern United States had lived in an increasingly segregated and racist society before migrating to Guatemala. In the late nineteenth century, state and local legislatures in the southern United States passed a flood of segregation laws that restricted opportunities for African Americans. At the same time, African Americans in the South witnessed and experienced an increase in racist violence. Lynching fluctuated noticeably within the different regions of individual states. In the Black Belt, lynching was a method of controlling black labor.[50] By the 1880s, violence against Southern blacks caused them to increasingly look outside their home regions for hope of a better life. A January 1881 newspaper article in New Orleans's *Weekly Louisianan* recounted why a group of African Americans from North Carolina had migrated north to Indiana. "Although nominally free since the war," wrote this group of emigrants, "our condition in the South was in fact one of servitude, and was each year becoming worse." Generally, the wages that white employers paid could purchase little more than poor food and clothing and "wretched" housing. In addition, the emigrants argued that racist North Carolina legislatures at the state and local level passed ordinances that openly discriminated against black citizens. At the same time, public officials administered other laws "as to have the same effect." In many regions of the state, African Americans who tried to purchase real estate found that upon making their final payment, the white seller would arrange some "legal technicality" that would prevent the black buyers from obtaining a deed to the property. When they took the seller to the state's white-controlled courts, judicial officials ruled against African American citizens, and the court costs were assessed against the black plaintiffs. Moreover, racist sheriffs in North Carolina seized upon every possible pretense "to send men of our race to the penitentiary," while they did nothing to white men who committed the same crimes for which the state punished blacks. African American migrants from the Tar Heel State recalled, "More and more each year we were deprived of our political rights, by fraud if not by violence. There was no security for our lives."[51]

The *Weekly Louisianan* also published an April 1881 article, entitled "Why They Emigrate," which contrasted European and Louisiana labor migration. The article reported that in March 1881 some 45,000 immigrants from Ireland, England, and Germany had come to the United States in search of greater security. It argued that North Americans wanted security and their own land too: "Like the Irishman and German, the colored laborer has the incidental desire to secure for himself a proper social consideration, and acknowledgement of equal political rights, improvement of education for his children which shall open to him all the avenues of industry, and all the grandees of official position." The article warned Louisiana sugar planters that unless they improved conditions for their "already insufficient" labor force, North American laborers, like Europeans, would opt for "inducements" in other countries to "better themselves." Some had already migrated to Indiana, Kansas, and New Mexico in search of "a climate adapted to their physical comfort, and a social condition satisfactory to their sense of personal rights." Determined black workers, the article warned, would travel even as far as Sonora, Michoacán, and Oaxaca, Mexico, or to Central America's Guatemala and Nicaragua, where they would "find, and make a Louisiana of their own."[52]

A 1904 circular sent out by an employment agency in New Orleans high-lighted the opportunities that Louisiana workers might pursue abroad. One labor recruiter's placard stated a wish for "White and Colored" workers. It promised that those who signed on would have the best opportunities, because Central America was the next booming region. When work was finished in Guatemala, the placard told laborers, they could move on to work in the Panama Canal Zone. It also informed potential recruits that after liv-ing in Guatemala they could find work on railroad construction projects in Honduras, Nicaragua, El Salvador, and Costa Rica. Those who preferred to "settle along the Guatemala railroad" would "have a good future before them," as "besides the forestry and coffee industry the fruit culture is quite a bonanza." Labor recruiters sought to attract men by telling them that Cen-tral America would be receiving an enormous infusion of investment capital in the banana industry: "From Puerto Barrios to Colon, there are thousands [of] acres of fruit land, awaiting for the industrious laborer to cultivate in ba-nanas especially, the best paying now in Central America. STEAMER LEAVES EVERY THURSDAY 9 A.M."[53]

Migrants' Stories

The biographical sketches of migrants who opted to go to Guatemala pro-vide insights into the variety of people who migrated there and why. The Collins family was perhaps among the first group of African Americans who immigrated to Guatemala. Henry Collins, born in Natchez, Mississippi, in 1879, immigrated to Guatemala with his mother and stepfather in 1894.[54] The contractor William T. Penney imported some seventy to eighty African American workers into Puerto Barrios on a weekly steamer from New Or-leans. According to Penney, "a great many of the men had their wives with them," making Penney's labor camp really look like "a fair sized village."[55]

As early as 1897, U.S. consular agents in the departments of Izabal and Alta Verapaz (the closest highland region to Puerto Barrios) began receiving complaints from black immigrants who claimed that they had been "enticed" to leave the United States for Guatemala "under false pretenses."[56] In 1898, many workers told the Livingston consular agent, Frank C. Dennis, that they had been "deceived into coming [to Guatemala]" by representatives of the Northern and Verapaz railroads in New Orleans.[57] Thomas Perry of Atlanta and John Green of Pensacola claimed that they had been "fooled" into leav-ing New Orleans for Puerto Barrios in 1898, when they were nineteen and eighteen years old, respectively. Both were consigned to working for the rail-roads.[58]

Simon Shine was born in 1880 in Montgomery, Alabama. He had traveled to Guatemala alone in 1894, when he was just fourteen. He had come under contract with the Northern Railroad, where he worked his way up from water boy to brakeman to fireman and finally to section foreman. Shine wrote of his years with the Northern: "I have been peaceable, industrious, frugal and law abiding. At the time that I quit the employment of the Railroad company, I had saved about fourteen thousand dollars of the money of the country."[59] African American George Martin, born in 1872, declared in a 1911 affidavit that he had emigrated from Jefferson County, Alabama, to Zacapa. The year of his arrival in Guatemala is unclear; he worked as a boilermaker, most likely for a railroad company. Louis P. McPherson, another African American, also came from Jefferson County, Alabama. He had migrated to Guatemala in 1895. He eventually married a Guatemalan woman and owned and operated a cattle ranch in Zacapa. McPherson became embroiled in a legal dispute with his Guatemalan father-in-law. The documents from the case detail his experience as an expatriate in Zacapa's North American colony. In a 1921 affidavit, he stated that he had left a wife and two small children behind in Alabama, whom he had not heard from in twenty-six years. "I have no definite intentions at present to return to the United States, as I have no money to pay for my passage," said McPherson. However, he stated that if he could go, he would go through the port of New Orleans and return "to Jefferson County, Alabama, to remain there indefinitely."[60]

In addition to the Department of Zacapa, black immigrants also settled in the port community in and around Puerto Barrios. Several black U.S. nationals in Puerto Barrios became property owners and entrepreneurs. Immigrant Sam Lee, for example, had been born in 1878 in Mississippi. In 1895, at the age of seventeen, he departed the United States for Guatemala. Those who knew him in Guatemala described him as "quite a shrewd fellow," and he was well-known throughout the "towns, farms, and camps along the railway" in the department of Izabal.[61] After marrying a Guatemalan national, Josefa Guzmán, Lee became a successful saloon operator and restaurateur in Puerto Barrios, as well as a merchant. Black immigrant Ira Lee Penix also operated a business in Puerto Barrios and married a Guatemalan national. Penix had been born in 1876 in Dallas County, Arkansas, and had arrived in Guatemala in 1894. By 1912, he owned and operated a store in Puerto Barrios and shared a home with a twenty-year-old Guatemalan national named Gumercinda Díaz.[62]

James W. Levy was one of several hundred workers who migrated to Guatemala in 1894 as a contract laborer. By 1913, Levy had organized a contracting business that performed the harsh job of grading roadbeds for the

International Railroad of Central America before the company could lay track on its line. Levy eventually married a Guatemalan woman, Margarita García, with whom he had at least one child. The couple rented a room in a boardinghouse in Guatemala City.While residing in Izabal, Levy acquired a reputation, according to U.S. consular agent Edward Reed, as a hustler who put in "most of his time gambling or around the gambling tables."[63]

In the summer of 1913 Levy organized a group of men to help him hold up the IRCA paymaster.[64] His cadre of would-be bandits consisted of, among others, African Americans William Brown, Andres Rodas (perhaps a Guatemalan), Harry Perking, James Taylor, Ricky Wadel, James Lowwiny, and Levy's wife, Margarita. In August of 1913 Levy and his gang ambushed and robbed Alberto Quiñoes, an IRCA paymaster traveling to Puerto Barrios. The paymaster and his guard were traveling by mule with the monthly employee salaries to IRCA labor camps. The robbery occurred in broad daylight. According to the police investigation of the robbery, the attack was "premeditated, and . . . the negroes for several days were waiting the passage of the strong box, hiding in the mountains, well knowing the time when the strong box leaves the camps to make the end of the month payments."[65] In the process of robbing Quiñoes, the gang shot and seriously wounded guard Francisco Valdez, who later died. To escape, they boarded a train from the Caribbean coast to the interior. They hid out in Guatemala City, "well provided with funds." Though the robbers managed to make a successful getaway with large amounts of Guatemalan currency and U.S. gold,[66] the day after their arrival in the capital, in exchange for fifty pesos, Renery Scott, an African American who apparently worked around the city's railroad station, led the police to the gang. City police officers surrounded the boardinghouse where the group of robbers was staying and arrested the men and their female accomplices. The police then extradited the lot to Izabal to stand trial for armed robbery and the murder of the guard, Francisco Valdez.[67]

Two soldiers and the IRCA's Quiñoes accompanied the suspects by train back to Puerto Barrios. Along the route, Quiñoes reported observing large numbers of African Americans who were "ready to free" Levy from the escort that guarded him. But in the end, the crowd made no effort to help Levy escape.[68] In assessing the probability of Levy's innocence, U.S. consular agent Edward Reed wrote, "Levy is without conscientious scruples, and is capable of committing the crime he is charged with. Let there be no doubt on this score. Often times the testimony of natives [Guatemalan nationals] is not satisfactory, but never so as that of the American negro."[69]

These biographical sketches reveal the diversity that existed among the North American migrants who traveled to Guatemala. They represented

Figure 1.1. United Fruit labor camp in Tela, Honduras

various age groups and ethnicities, and they had had various life experiences in the United States prior to migrating. As we shall see, many workers had participated in radical movements in the southern United States, the Panama Canal Zone, and in other parts of the Americas before going to Guatemala. Their travels, at home and abroad, seem to have contributed to the radicalization of the workers prior to their arrival in Guatemala.[70]

A Tradition of Labor Radicalism and Poverty

In the late nineteenth century, according to the historian Daniel Letwin, African American miners in Alabama "took the initiative in mobilizing at places where union structures had lapsed." In mining towns where African American miners outnumbered whites, they could fill the majority of union leadership positions. "Interracial cooperation remained evident in localized strikes, even amid the use of black strikebreakers," notes Letwin. He adds, "Where black miners did lead the way in labor battles, whites were urged not to spurn them." Both black and white miners viewed each other not in terms of black and white, but as "genuine" as opposed to "scab" miners.[71]

Unlike the dockworkers and miners, the railroad brotherhoods made no attempt at interracialism in the late nineteenth century. Eric Arnesen argues that "the racial beliefs of white railroaders proved an insurmountable barrier separating white from black.... White workers went well beyond excluding blacks from their brotherhoods: they actively campaigned for restrictions on black employment and blacks' wholesale elimination from jobs in the railway operating crafts."[72] Arnesen goes on to say that in the 1880s the Knights of Labor served to unite black and white workers, "however tentatively," in many regions of the South. The Knights supported a tolerant and cooperative character that fostered, in Arneson's words, "an unprecedented if short-lived interracial solidarity." During the 1880s, the Knights became substantially more popular in the South. In addition, New Orleans was reputed to have the South's most organized and powerful workforce.[73] Such newspapers as the *Weekly Louisianan* provide evidence that the workers from New Orleans and the sugar parishes of Louisiana who traveled to Central America were already familiar with radical labor movements.

In April 1880, for instance, the *Weekly Louisianan* reported on the outbreak of labor strikes in Louisiana's Saint Charles and Saint John parishes. The governor of Louisiana dispatched state militiamen to repress the strikes. During the same month, striking laborers playing music and displaying a banner marched in protest up to the sugar plantation region of Donaldsonville, Louisiana. The following month, black plantation workers in Ascension Parish went on strike for higher wages. Soon, other hands refused to answer the bell calling workers out to the fields. One group of workers in Ascension Parish "formed a gang, all mounted on horses," which "marched two-by-two" to a nearby plantation where workers were ignoring the work stoppage. The strikers continued on to other plantations "and compelled laborers there to suspend work under pain of violence should they refuse to comply with the demand."[74] Similar movements occurred in others parts of the South. Black and white workers on the docks in New Orleans, in logging camps and sawmills in East Texas, and in the mines of Alabama "built organizations that defied southern racial protocol and challenged the prerogatives being fastened on the region by leading men of the New South."[75]

Similar labor radicalism existed in Central America. Labor radicalism among migrant workers in Central America dates back as far as 1853, when a group of North American workers of Irish descent from New Orleans organized a work stoppage until their employers improved health conditions and wages on a railroad construction project in Panama. Eventually, local authorities used armed force to end the strike. The episode persuaded contractors to discontinue the importing of large numbers of U.S. workers, "in order to avoid such delays in construction or the threat of having to pay higher wage rates."[76] Some thirty years later, in 1883, employees of the Panama Railroad Company would go out on strike to demand higher wages. With the support of some unnamed North American labor organizations, the striking workers would remain resolute and achieve their demands.

In the late nineteenth century, U.S. railroad brotherhoods made serious attempts to wrest power from railroad owners, particularly in the years

1877, 1885–86, and 1894.[77] In the words of historian Eric Arnesen, "Bitterly fought railroad strikes collapsed in the face of massive corporate, state, and federal repression, and failed strikers often found themselves effectively blacklisted out of the industry."[78] At the turn of the century, the traveler Nevin O. Winter found that it was the North Americans who controlled the engineer and conductor jobs in the Central American railroad industry, "many of them . . . having been discharged from American [rail]roads for various offences." Some of these laborers had migrated to Central America "by a succession of steps on Mexican [rail]roads." The traveler Arthur Ruhl referred to the Guatemalan Caribbean coast city of Zacapa as a "dreary outpost of Industrialism" inhabited by West Indians, Guatemalans, Honduran, and North American railroad workers.[79]

Migrants from the United States to Guatemala in the last years of the nineteenth century were also likely to have experienced—and perhaps to have been motivated by—extreme poverty. The United States experienced its worst economic crisis of the century between 1893 and 1897. The depression produced business collapses, enormous wage cuts, and deepening poverty across the country. Up to a fifth of the nation's industrial workforce may have been jobless in the winter of 1893–94. The depression struck the labor movement extremely hard. According to Arnesen: "The craft unions that made up the young American Federation of Labor lost considerable ground, as employers successfully took the offensive against union work rules and wages."[80] In Louisiana, the daily rate for unskilled labor fell from $1.50 to $1.00 between 1883 and 1888. During the 1890s, the daily wages paid to skilled workers fell miserably, too. In New Orleans, people were so poor that merchants had to divide the nickel, which served as the common currency of the day, into brass tags known as "quarties," to permit smaller purchases. Both whites and blacks flooded the almshouses and benevolent institutions, "of which Louisiana had more inmates than other Southern states."[81] Destitute whites constituted the majority of those receiving handouts. During the early 1890s, over five thousand received rations in the form of dinners and lunches for the homeless.

By the end of the nineteenth century, a sizable portion of the population of New Orleans was living in abject poverty, as were many residents of other American cities.[82] During the depression of the 1890s, coal miners in Jefferson County, Alabama, also experienced hard times, finding it difficult to locate regular employment and sometimes working only once or twice per week.[83] It was in this economic climate that the North American railroad contractors in Guatemala hired labor recruiters to work in Southern port cities. Sources do not reveal the fees labor agencies or their subcontractors received for their services.[84]

Dating back to the colonial period, the elite members of Guatemalan society had viewed people of African descent as exploitable and expendable, at the same time that they feared the increasing insubordination of enslaved Africans and the growing number of free black communities. After Independence and the abolition of slavery in 1825, Guatemalan views of blacks changed very little. Late-nineteenth-century sources indicate that the government of Guatemala was loath to attract black emigrants to the country, but Guatemalan officials and North American contractors alike acknowledged that the recruitment of black contract laborers was a necessity for the construction of the railroads that that began in the mid-1880s as an effort to improve the marketing of Guatemalan coffee and to expand the banana industry. Thus, black workers were recruited primarily in the United States and Jamaica, and these workers, from diverse backgrounds and experiences, arrived in Guatemala in the hope of advancing their prospects through hard work. As the next chapter will show, most of them were systematically taken advantage of by the labor agents, by company supervisors, and by the Guatemalan officials whom they encountered.

2

Race, Resistance, and Revolution in the Late Nineteenth Century

Completing the Northern Railroad required laborers to be imported from abroad and coerced to remain doing difficult work in extremely inhospitable conditions. The Guatemalan state assisted its multinational partners in enticing black workers to the Caribbean coast, often under false pretences, and forcing them to remain in debt servitude to white employers. Workers who attempted to complain to state authorities or to run away, as well as those who committed real or perceived crimes, usually suffered abuse at the hands of state officials. Yet even in the early years, this diverse coastal labor force was far from passive: when the railroad project strained the Guatemalan state's budget beyond its capacity during an economic depression, a revolution ensued, and in its wake, the workers on the Caribbean coast united in a strike in 1898 to demand better wages and working conditions.

"It was Rough": How Labor Agents Swindled Immigrants

Labor agents often used unscrupulous tactics to get workers to board steamships for Guatemala without the workers' knowledge of the ships' actual destination or the working conditions they would endure.[1] U.S. citizens Frederick Scott and Samuel Hills describe their experience with labor agents in an unattributed newspaper article entitled "It Was Rough," dated approximately May 1897. The labor agents, wrote Scott and Hills, had "told falsehoods and enticed us over there by saying we would have decent food and good treatment. We had the worst food imaginable. We were beaten and our lives threatened." A second newspaper clipping dealt with a case in Monroe, Louisiana. It described a May 1897 district criminal court grand jury indictment of labor agents J. H. Randolph and W. M. Sims. According to the article, the grand jury indicted the two men on charges of "kidnapping negros and sending them to work on a railroad in Guatemala." The presiding judge set each man's bond at $500.[2]

Coercion and fraud brought some workers to Guatemala, but others went simply because they believed there were better opportunities there than in their home countries. A U.S. consular agent explained in a letter to his superior, "Laborers whether white or black come here expecting often times to get their passage to a warm climate and be able to live without work—eat fruit, and sleep in the woods." Many workers were interested in migrating to Guatemala "to better their fortunes in a new land."[3] Indeed, in January 1885 the captain of the Guatemala-bound steamer *Blanche Henderson* reported that when his ship docked in New Orleans, more men crowded the entrance to the vessel than there were places for them. Crewmembers had "to drive them off the ship with clubs, and in spite of this twelve stowaways appeared after they got out to sea."[4] Though coercion was hardly necessary in most cases, the fraudulent recruiting tactics that influenced most migrants to decide to travel to Guatemala meant that they could not truly know what they were signing on for.

The Region of Babel

Most often, recruiters and contractors advanced high-interest loans to workers to pay for their steamship fare. In exchange, workers consigned themselves to work off the advance at specific work sites.[5] Upon arrival in Guatemala, the workers received a less-than-cordial welcome from employers and state officials alike. According to William B. Lyons and J. C. Watts of Ohio, armed Guatemalan soldiers taunted and insulted the new arrivals as they escorted them to their living quarters on the island of Livingston.[6] In 1881, Livingston had a little over a hundred inhabitants; most of them earned their livelihood from fishing. However, the construction of the Northern Railroad changed "the sleepy hamlet into the busy haunt of contractors and laborers." By 1887, the island's population had increased to about two thousand, most of them Garifuna but a smaller number of them Mayan or Latin American families.[7]

While some immigrants disembarked at the port of Livingston, others arrived at Puerto Barrios, also on the Caribbean coast of Guatemala. Since the start of the Northern Railroad project, the population of Puerto Barrios had risen substantially. In November 1894 the port town had some four hundred homes and a modern hospital suitable for up to fifty patients. The city looked like a construction zone, with railroad industry equipment, building materials, and rusted locomotives all over the place.[8]

The influx of foreign laborers resulted in an ethnically diverse lowland workforce.[9] Employment opportunities in Barrios attracted workers from around the world, who spoke many different languages. When traveler Nevin O. Winter visited the Caribbean coast port, he heard "Spanish, German,

French, English, Chinese, and the unintelligible gibberish of the Carib [the Garifuna]" spoken by members of the port's small population.[10] Miguel Angel Asturias, a Guatemalan Nobel Laureate in Literature, described Puerto Barrios as a place with the "mystery of languages" and the "confusion of the Tower of Babel."[11] In 1895, among the workers that Northern Railroad officials hired, only 25 percent of them spoke Spanish.[12]

Like the workers, foreign capitalists and mid-level managers also came to Guatemala in hopes of capitalizing on the expansion of U.S. interests in Central America. The majority of them were white, North American men between twenty and forty years old and from upper-class families. They were generally only five to ten years older than their employees.[13] Born in 1865 in Quebec, Canada, William T. Penney, for example, had started his career with the Phoenix Bridge Company at the age of fourteen. He worked for the company until his twenty-second birthday, at which time he had formed a partnership with Harry Givler. Penney and Givler started out as bridge contractors in Mexico and maintained their partnership until the death of Givler. Penney then managed the business on his own, relocating his base of operations to Guatemala City in the late 1890s. While in Guatemala, he became identified with the construction of the Northern Railroad.[14]

Among those important people associated with some of the earliest U.S.-owned multinational corporations operating in Guatemala was Silvanus Miller. Miller imported workers for railroad construction projects in the departments of Zacapa and Izabal. Martin Roberts and A. C. Ham imported an estimated five hundred workers to build railroad lines in the same departments.[15] The Guatemalan railroad industry, which was financed by foreign investment capital and Guatemalan public funds, was a complex enterprise in which the government employed both Guatemalan nationals and foreigners. Several men important to its operation were José M. Amerlinck, director engineer and technical director of the Northern Railroad; L. P. Pennypacker, inspector engineer of the Northern Railroad; and F. García, general superintendent of the Northern Railroad.[16]

Contractor William T. Penney wrote that it cost a contractor "$38.00 each" to import workers from New Orleans. That included the roughly $13 cost of passage, "the money paid the labor agent in New Orleans[,] together with blanket and mosquito bar [nets] furnished each man."[17] When a laborer agreed to take an advance from his employer to cover costs, therefore, he was paying for much more than the actual $13 cost of passage to Guatemala. The advance most often included the cost of mosquito netting, clothes, and blankets, all of which employers sold out of the company's commissaries at inflated prices. They could get away with such exploitative tactics because they monopolized the sale of virtually all essential items. In addition, employers often paid wages to workers in commissary goods.[18]

As early as 1884, U.S. consular agent James F. Sarg found that workers on the Caribbean coast could not pay their debts because, he wrote, the "contractors do not pay in cash, but in checks, which are not exchangeable into money, and are only received at the contractor's store in exchange for goods" sold at exorbitant prices. Even after six months of employment, workers on the Caribbean coast often found themselves still indebted to company officials. As a result, large numbers of workers ran away from their position of debt peonage.[19]

Many of those who remained seem to have formed relationships with local women. Penney, who constructed new bridges at some of the earliest modernization projects in Central America and Mexico, described labor camps in Guatemala as being occupied by as many as ninety men and their wives. In general, however, young unmarried men resided in the labor camps without wives. During the period under study, the length of relationships between foreign men and Guatemalan women varied from short-term to long-term. By the turn of the century, it was common for workers who had arrived on the Caribbean coast in the 1890s to have established relationships and families with Caribbean coast women. Still others carried on short-term relationships with Guatemalan women.[20] In the late nineteenth century, the Caribbean coast had a gender disparity that encouraged miscegenation between foreign-born black men and Guatemalan women. Many of these women migrated to the Caribbean coast, where they worked as domestics, operated portable kitchens, and worked in bars and brothels.[21]

American citizenship registration records indicate that some U.S. workers abandoned their North American families and married Guatemalan nationals. Wives left behind also formed extramarital relationships.[22] Workers who came to Guatemala at a young age tended to become acculturated with the people of the Caribbean coast in all their attachments. Cohabitation relationships with children bonded workers to the geographical location of their children's maternal family. The few workers documented as starting families with Guatemalan women for whom we have adequate documentation stayed in Guatemala the rest of their lives. This was the case both for those who formally married Guatemalans and for those who entered into common-law marriages. Family formation represented one of the many signs of one's integration and acculturation into the Guatemalan Caribbean world. But those workers who left behind wives and children in the United States most often returned to them, and thus did not fully integrate into Guatemalan society.[23]

Starting in the 1890s, the population of Puerto Barrios boomed as a result of renewed efforts to complete the Northern Railroad. The railroad facilitated the construction of new homes, schools, shops, hotels, restaurants, cantinas, courthouses, and jails. The construction boom provided additional job opportunities for unskilled laborers. In addition to controlling jobs in construction, immigrant workers controlled many of the waterfront jobs at the turn of the century.[24] Highly skilled artisans, such as cooks, blacksmiths, boilermakers, carpenters, plumbers, electricians, and mechanics, also found work in Puerto Barrios.[25] Boilermaker George Martin from Jefferson County, Alabama, for example, earned a good living in the railroad industry because the boilers on trains constantly needed repair or replacement. Martin, who was a black U.S. national, indicated that he worked for Penney at Puerto Barrios.[26] Here, it became clear to him that the best opportunities in Guatemala came first to the people with training and white skin.[27]

Crime and Punishment

Local officials stereotyped black laborers as lawless and dangerous. As a result, black migrant men were frequently subjected to racist attacks by civilians and state officials alike. In a February 1897 letter to the Guatemalan minister of government and justice, Zacapa governor Elias Estrada described members of Zacapa's black immigrant working class as violent and lawless. That same month, a municipal judge in Zacapa told the minister of government and justice that before him came black men that Zacapa police arrested for robbery, homicides, and attempted rape.[28]

As government subcontractors, railroad contractors could and did use Guatemalan soldiers to enforce their agreement with workers. The departments of Izabal and Zacapa each had strategically placed fortified garrisons manned by poorly paid soldiers and military officers. The soldiers had the responsibility to defend the nation and police its departments.[29] Most often, the line between civic and military officials was blurred, and *jefe politicos* (or governors) and their subordinates customarily used a multitude of methods to illegally supplement their meager government salaries. Civilian and military authorities did their best to financially exploit both blacks and Latin Americans. Local authorities received a bribe for forcing native Americans into work gangs, to be used by those in need of unskilled laborers.[30] Employers also used soldiers to hunt down black runaways and to stand guard at worksites. This protected both the state and the employers against losses due to runaway indebted workers.[31] Soldiers forced runaways they caught to pay them a $5-per-day fee, while departmental commandants on occasion forced them to pay about $40 in Guatemalan currency.[32] Moreover, the state and employers treated railroad laborers like convict laborers, posting guards at worksites and sometimes whipping apprehended runaways. Employers and state officials operated the Caribbean coast like a penal colony. One laborer claimed that the coast was "just like Siberia, only hot instead of cold."[33]

Workers often died shortly after arriving, or they lived out the remainder of their lives with diseases. As a consequence of employer neglect, many became deathly ill. Some attempted to flee rather than remain in the unhealthy railroad camps, in which dysentery, yellow fever, and other diseases were rampant.[34] Contractors justified the harsh treatment of workers by claiming that they paid and fed their employees well and that they could always get men when others suffered labor shortages. This was far from the truth.

Sick and Diseased

The inhumane treatment of railroad workers in the 1890s was nothing new. In fact, the workers' struggle with employers and the state to improve their working and living conditions dated back to at least 1884.[35] In a January 15, 1885, letter, Henry C. Hall of the U.S. legation in Central America notified members of the U.S. State Department of alarming reports submitted by Livingston consular agent Sarg. Sarg had received word from the Izabal hospital staff about American casualties in Guatemala's war against tropical disease on the Caribbean coast. After investigating the matter, he reported to the legation about the appalling conditions he had discovered. Sarg's reports provide detailed descriptions of the working and living conditions the railroad crews had to tolerate, and of the many ways they did so. Hall informed his superior that a number of the railroad workers, who had come from New Orleans, were penniless and slowly dying from sickness and disease. As a result, Hall requested that the Navy send a vessel and men to fully investigate the reports of the consular agent and to rescue and return the destitute Americans to New Orleans.

Between three hundred and five hundred laborers were unemployed and stranded in Izabal.[36] The earliest workers fared so poorly because company managers consigned them to malaria-infested swamp areas. Workers slept in canvas tents full of holes in swampy areas. In one region of Izabal, employers buried some seventy black U.S. workers. Some had died of tropical diseases, while others had died trying to escape debt peonage.[37] In a December 1885 letter, white North American employee Con Hickey reported: "I have been kept at work from October 30th until December 21, had to build a shelter for myself and was served with bad and damaged provisions for which I was made to pay a high price." After Hickey contracted malaria, the employer he worked for took the cost of medicine and hospital care out of his wages.[38] When Sarg visited the hospital in Izabal, many workers complained to him about horrid living and working conditions. They chiefly complained about the poor quality of the meat they received and about provisions that made them sick.[39] They had tried to file a complaint against their employers with the local *comandante*, but none of them spoke Spanish, and they could not find an interpreter. An interpreter probably would not have helped, as the *comandante* seems only to have been interested in relieving workers of what little money they earned. Besides, contractors obligated departmental authorities to assist in the task of keeping unskilled laborers on the job so that construction projects could be completed on time.[40]

By Christmas 1884, some railroad workers were beginning to weigh the choice of returning to their countries or enduring the conditions in Guatemala. At the beginning of January 1885, Sarg reported that a group of sick and stranded workers had boarded the New Orleans-bound steamship *Ellie Knight* at Puerto Barrios and Livingston.[41] At the end of the same month, a large number of workers departed for Belize, prompting British authorities there to strictly enforce vagrancy laws. Officials in Belize would give workers streaming across the border from Guatemala the choice of either working on state construction projects or spending time in jail doing prison labor for violating the country's vagrancy laws.[42] Indeed, being used as prison labor was a constant complaint among workers on the Caribbean coast of Guatemala.

In March 1885, the commander of the U.S. naval ship *Swatara*, J. C. Wiltse, docked his ship at the port of Livingston.[43] Wiltse recorded in the ship's logbook the names of thirty-three stranded laborers who boarded his ship for New Orleans. He used the Jim Crow identification "colored American" to clearly identify six of the men listed as black U.S. nationals. The rest of the passengers included fifteen white U.S. nationals, seven Germans, three Englishmen, one Irishman, and one French citizen.[44] The *Swatara* proceeded from Livingston to Puerto Barrios to pick up forty additional passengers of various nationalities.[45]

Grievances and Revolution

During the early years, white U.S. nationals and a few white Latin American professionals monopolized the better-paying jobs in the Latin American railroad industry. U.S. managers and engineers almost exclusively supervised lower-class whites and non-white track workers. The white U.S. general manager of the Guatemalan Railroad, F. G. Williamson, believed his experience with various classes of workers justified the company's racialized hiring practices. He argued that white workers sent from New Orleans "could not stand the climate and, anyhow, did not come here to work." He also claimed, "Blacks are inferior in average intelligence to the Jamaican negroes," and "The American negro is lazier and more vicious altho' stronger than the Jamaican." Williamson's desire was to hire only Jamaicans as track workers.[46]

White North American employers used a complex formula to pay unskilled workers. Some unskilled workers earned wages under the supervision of company managers. Others formed their own crews and negotiated subcontracts for laying track in the thick jungle sections. This task system allowed workers greater autonomy in selecting their coworkers and salaries. However, contractors still maintained a monopoly over medical care, housing, and the sale of merchandise.[47] Most employees had no available alternative in these isolated, swampy regions than to live in company housing. They also had no alternative in these same isolated environments than to purchase basic necessities from company commissaries. Without the commissaries, the laborers would have been in an unsustainable situation.[48]

To compound their already precarious existence, laborers frequently did not receive wages at all. From 1897, the growth of the Guatemalan economy gradually began to slow, and the national treasury shrank. The financial burden of constructing the Northern Railroad threw the Guatemalan economy and the Reyna Barrios administration into a tailspin.[49] Excessive levying of taxes to finance the military and the railroad helped cause a national depression. The practically bankrupt government did not have the funds necessary to pay contractors, and therefore contractors did not pay their workers.[50]

As the situation worsened, the administration's political opponents eagerly exploited the crisis, with outcries against mismanagement and calls for revolutionary change. These opponents included leading Conservative Party members Próspero Morales (minister of war under Reyna Barrios and later the governor of San Marcos), General José León Castillo (the governor of Chiquimula), Daniel Fuentes Barrios (the governor of Quiché), and Feliciano Aguilar.[51] By 1897, Reyna Barrios's authoritarian control of Guatemalan politics and the continued economic burden of the Northern Railroad helped ignite revolutionary movements in the western and eastern regions of the republic.[52] By March of 1897, workers were very unhappy and were openly protesting delays in receiving their weekly pay. José M. Amerlinck, superintendent of the Northern Railroad, noted, "If the situation continues worsening the discontent will translate into acts of violence and crime against the property of this company that would be very lamentable."[53]

At the same time that the railroad workers struggled with U.S. contractors and the Guatemalan government for back wages, opposition to Reyna Barrios's increasingly authoritarian regime was building in the National Assembly in Guatemala City and throughout the various departments. In May 1897, Reyna Barrios grew tired of the National Assembly members' unwillingness to support his initiatives. He suspended the legislature and consolidated national power in his own hands. In addition, he imprisoned his most outspoken critics. Reyna Barrios sought to consolidate his control over the country's political process, extend his term as president, complete the Northern Railroad, and gratify his personal need for power.[54]

Just before Reyna Barrios took office, the National Assembly had passed a law prohibiting the constitutional reelection of the chief of state. Presidents before Reyna Barrios had established a tradition of holding on to power as long as possible and by any means necessary. Now that legislation prohibited such traditions, opposition forces mobilized against Reyna Barrios's attempt to stay in power illegally. By the end of May 1897, Reyna Barrios had acquired the popular title of "dictator" and had stirred many toward revolutionary opposition to his administration.[55] Rebel leaders, such as General José León Castillo, argued that Reyna Barrios's economic policies had destabilized Guatemala's economy. Castillo faulted Reyna Barrios for "questionable negotiations" with companies in which the president had personal business interests, "an increase in the public debt never seen before," and "the centralization of autocratic power."[56]

In the east, the revolution began at the end of September 1897 when a group of Guatemaltecos met across the border in El Salvador. Among the revolutionary junta were General Castillo, General José N. Rodríguez, Rosendo Santa Cruz, Mateo Paz Pinto, Colonel Salvador Cuellar, and General Monterroso. After crossing the border into Guatemala, Castillo and Monterroso led an October attack on the departments of Izabal and Zacapa.[57] Rebel forces took control of Puerto Barrios and the Northern Railroad. Shortly thereafter, Generals Monterroso, Castillo, Rodríguez, and their rebel forces captured the capital of Zacapa. They freed all the prisoners, many of whom were African American railroad men. Castillo then departed for another department, while Monterroso remained to control the capital. Rebel forces ransacked the capital until government reinforcements overran them and General Rodríguez deserted and sided with the triumphant government troops.[58] In recounting the events in Zacapa, General Castillo wrote: "After the defection of General Rodríguez, we attacked the Zacapa plaza when we now had only 200 men of which 150 fought. The attack was victorious, but the superior numbers of the enemy obligated us to retreat without abandoning our weapons of warfare."[59]

After the rebels retreated and relinquished their control over Zacapa, the Guatemalan government accused North American John H. Ulses, a white barroom and gambling house manager, of collaborating with the revolutionaries. Ulses's written testimony, along with reports from U.S. investigators, provide a detailed account of events in Zacapa on the eve of the revolution.[60] Ulses claimed: "I had nothing to do with the revolution but the revolutionists forced me to work on bringing out archives to burn. . . . Wallace Dice [a] negro prisoner—also another named Barley were forced to help burn papers of the Court House." Consular reports on events before the arrival of the rebel forces reveal that Zacapa authorities had arrested Ulses after a dispute between him and his landlord. The dispute occurred when Ulses opened a bar and gambling house at El Rancho, in the department of Zacapa. Ulses's unnamed Guatemalan landlord soon became "disgusted with the disreputable crowd, that made night hideous" and took legal action to evict him. An armed conflict erupted between the two men, in which Ulses shot his landlord twice. After being imprisoned, "he was liberated by the insurgents, and made a line for the court house with the other prisoners to burn his sentence, thinking thereby to wipe out all evidence in his case." As the story went, "When an alarm that Government troops were coming arrived, he started for Gualán [in the department of Zacapa] to kill Williams, the American he had an account to settle." He then turned to rebel leaders and proposed the idea of recruiting unemployed African Americans for the revolutionary army under General Monterroso.[61]

Consular agent Dennis reported that the U.S. citizens had joined the revolutionary forces and "accepted arms and uniforms" of their own free will. The workers served the rebels "as guides to yards where horses and mules could be stolen." They also joined the rebels "in the robbery of the towns." Many of the workers who had turned rebels died when government troops, under the command of a General Toledo, overran their lines during a pitched battle. According to Dennis, the men "received a dollar silver per day" for their services as mercenaries. For men still waiting for government funds to pay contractors and then employees, the wages were "sufficient inducement."[62]

Joining the revolutionary forces also provided the men with an opportunity to legitimize criminal activity in Zacapa. Two gangs of men counted on the "arrival of revolutionists to sack and burn villages and wreak vengeance on officials and whoever they had any feud with."[63] An African American worker called "Mule" seems to have taken an organizing role among those who joined the insurgents. In the end, Guatemalan military officials had Mule executed for leading the African American contingency that "fought in the ranks of the revolutionists."[64]

Shortly after the battle in Zacapa, the war ended. However, a foreigner named Otto Zollinger assassinated Reyna Barrios on a February night in 1898. Once again, Guatemalans witnessed a violent transition to its next head of state. President Manuel Estrada Cabrera used the threat of violence to manipulate members of the Guatemalan National Assembly into supporting his appointment as Reyna Barrios's successor.[65]

In the final analysis, some of the workers who joined the rebels were prisoners who supported the revolutionary cause as an act of solidarity with the group who liberated them. Others joined because the rebel leaders provided a paycheck, food, and an opportunity to loot towns and mete out revenge against employers and the state. The motives of Guatemalans fighting in these destructive civil wars that regularly occurred during the late nineteenth century differed little from the motives of some of these opportunistic railroad workers. Above all, the employees were angry with the multinational corporations and the state because both were complicit in not paying them on time or at all.[66]

"The Workers are Disgusted:" The 1898 Railroad Strike

Political instability in 1897 exacerbated Guatemala's economic woes, which in turn created large numbers of unpaid and unemployed workers and social unrest in Zacapa. In July 1898, Guatemalan minister of development Juan Paz Tomas notified the minister of government and justice that the contractor of the Northern Railroad complained of observing a certain hostility from the Zacapa judge against the employees of the company. He added that, as this was a national development project that had to continue, "protection [was] needed from all the authorities."[67]

The problem stemmed from large numbers of unemployed black workers in and around the capital of Zacapa, who turned to crime in order to acquire basic necessities. As a result of these desperate workers' behavior, Zacapa authorities began to hold all blacks in contempt and indiscriminately arrested railroad employees in good standing. Authorities brutalized and mistreated black workers, who claimed their innocence, protested, or resisted arrest. In the conflict, employers sided with their employees and called upon national officials to curb the behavior of local Zacapa officials. In this instance, assistance from a company patron provided the workers with enough leverage to get branches of the national government in Guatemala City to provide them with "protection . . . from all the authorities."[68] In September 1898, consular agent Dennis reported a number of "robberies and abuses . . . mostly if not entirely confined to the Zacapa section," where "there are about 350 to 400 American citizens, more or less in destitute conditions."[69]

By the end of September, skilled and unskilled railroad workers in Gualán, Zacapa, refused to work without assurances that they would be paid. The men demanded advance pay before they would return to work, forcing U.S. contractors to suspend all work until the Guatemalan government could guarantee their wages. From Gualán, L. P. Pennybacker telegrammed the director of the Northern Railroad that "the workers are on strike in the Gualán shops and also the employees of the service trains." On the second day of the strike, Pennybacker reported, "I have communicated with the Governor and the guards in the train stations. The workers in Gualán are a bit disgusted today, but I believe that nothing will occur."[70]

The strike proved effective. On October 1, 1898, the governor of Zacapa notified Pennypacker that the money needed to pay the workers would arrive shortly. The railroad workers in Zacapa remained off the job, however.[71] A few days later, the mechanics demanded back wages from the month of July through the end of September 1898. Railroad contractor Robert H. May explained to U.S. State Department officials, "I will of course be unable to accede to their demands until other funds are forthcoming from Guatemala."[72]

By mid-October, Guatemalan nationals such as Enancio DeLeón grew suspicious of the attention of both the striking workers and their employers. This was because "public rumor" had it that the foreign contractors and the workers had conspired together to extort the Guatemalan government for more money. In addition, the two groups allegedly had conspired to exclude Guatemalan nationals from control of the railroad industry. The government appointed a commission to investigate the allegations and to consider the complete nationalization of the Northern Railroad. In an affidavit, DeLeón declared of May, "[he] opposes the delivery of the line to the commission of the government, alleging fictitious protests that are not justification" only so that "North Americans nationals and other parties" can monopolize the line.[73]

The commission's finding influenced the government's "forcible possession of the Northern Railroad" by the end of October 1898.[74] As late as the end of November 1898, May was receiving "daily calls" from former railroad employees demanding payment "for the month of October up to the 20th, the date of [his] forceful ejection." The workers asked him, "To whom are we to look for the payment of work done during the period that elapsed from the time of the strike among the mechanics up to the date of the ejection of Mr. May?" The government hired another U.S. contractor, Martin Roberts, to replace May. One of Roberts's first actions was firing a number of the striking workers who were "very persistent in their demands."[75] In 1900, an unidentified plaintiff filed a civil suit against May in the Guatemalan superior court at Puerto Barrios. Guatemalan law called for May to be detained to ensure his presence at the appointed court date and compelled May to authorize a "power of attorney to represent him in the suit." U.S. officials suspected that Guatemalan authorities in the capital had sent "private instructions" to local officials in Izabal to take "arbitrary and illegal action" against May in revenge for the shutdown of the Northern Railroad during the 1898 labor strike.[76]

The shared experience of struggling against dishonest labor recruiters and violently oppressive employers backed by the Guatemalan state played an important role in mobilizing the diverse labor pool on Guatemala's Caribbean coast during the 1898 strike. The most interesting aspect of the 1898 strike, however, may have been the brief collaboration between foreign labor and foreign capital against the Guatemalan state. The workers sent a settlement proposal to the Ministry of Development, which the government rejected in favor of arbitrating the dispute. The strike did not end until the government replaced May with Roberts. Those workers who were not fired returned to work at the end of the strike. By 1900, however, the majority of the line workers and some of the shop workers in Gualán who had supported the strike had taken better-paying jobs elsewhere. Consequently, Roberts found himself in the middle of a labor shortage that made it difficult to maintain the line in good condition. In response, he turned to Guatemalans, Mexicans, and other workers to meet the railroad's labor demands.[77]

3

Race Relations on the Early-Twentieth-Century Caribbean Frontier

Between 1912 and 1914, UFCO employed more than 4,000 workers: about 3,500 were of African descent, 500 were Latin Americans, and 300 were white North Americans in high-paying positions.[1] West Indians (particularly Jamaicans) came to dominate the landscape of the banana enclaves and the small towns near the provincial centers along the Northern Railroad.[2] According to some scholars, UFCO officials strategically imported diverse groups to undermine working-class solidarity.[3] As a result, numerous bloody fights and small riots broke out between Guatemalan and Jamaican plantation workers.[4] Violence involving alcohol, dice, guns, and knives was endemic in the railroad towns of Izabal, and especially in Zacapa, so perhaps it is not surprising that it was also common on the UFCO banana plantations located in Izabal. UFCO workers lived within a Jim Crow company enclave, where black and Hispanic laborers were housed in the same vicinity in barracks. Meanwhile, the white bosses lived in more luxurious, segregated houses. The Caribbean coast was a tough place to live: it was a violent, lawless, frontier region where largely single men worked, drank, and gambled with reckless abandon. This chapter explores interethnic conflict on the early-twentieth-century coast of Guatemala, considering how it was exacerbated by a shift in the composition of UFCO's workforce, local officials' biased treatment, and the nativist policies of the Guatemalan government.

Changing the Complexion of the Northern Railroad

By 1900, the railroad workforce had begun to undergo an ethnic and national transformation in which Guatemalan and Mexican workers replaced white and black U.S. workers and Jamaicans. The impetus for this change was twofold: Guatemalan nationals pushed for unskilled and skilled jobs on the railroad, and some foreign nationals left to pursue better opportunities both inside and outside of Guatemala.

Affidavits taken during police investigations provide detailed accounts of several workers' transitions from railroad employees to property owners or small-scale entrepreneurs. African American Simon Shine worked for thirteen years for the Northern before he saved enough money to become the owner of a boardinghouse in the capital, Zacapa. In 1907, at the age of twenty-seven, Shine operated a barbershop, bar, and gambling room with his Guatemalan mistress on property that he owned. The couple earned enough money to pay all the required monthly municipal fees to operate a business in the gambling and liquor trade.[5] African American Sam Lee operated a similar business in Puerto Barrios. Born in 1878 in Canton, Mississippi, Lee had departed the South for Guatemala at age seventeen, arriving in the country in 1895 as a railroad worker. In time, he married a Guatemalan woman and saved enough wages to operate a saloon and restaurant in Puerto Barrios. Lee also became a merchant trader.[6]

Available evidence suggests that West Indians similarly transitioned out of jobs with UFCO and IRCA once they had saved enough money to move on. In 1908, for instance, Jamaican Joseph Delatorre planned on returning to the West Indies to spend the money he had saved while working in Zacapa for the Northern Railroad, which paid him a good wage. Unfortunately, someone robbed both his clothing and his money from his room in a Zacapa boardinghouse shortly before his departure from the Caribbean coast. The police arrested a man who lived in the same boardinghouse for the crime.[7]

UFCO Expands Inland

The reshaping of the coastal labor force also reflected deliberate government policy. By September 1900, Minor Keith's Central American Improvement Company (CAICO) had purchased the rights to the Northern Railroad, taking over control of the line from the Guatemalan government and its contractor, Martin Roberts. The final deal provided Keith with government subsidies and 57,000 acres on which to plant bananas. As Keith was the founder and largest shareholder of both UFCO and CAICO, the agreement signaled UFCO's first expansion into the Guatemalan interior.

Government concessions gave Keith the right to operate the line for ten years, with exclusive control over all profits in exchange for repairing and extending the existing line to Guatemala City within thirty-three months. By awarding the contract, Reyna Barrios's successor, Manuel Estrada Cabrera, signaled his belief that the completion of the Northern Railroad was more important than who owned it. The agreement to allow a foreign interest to operate the railroad line ceded much of the government's control over Guatemala and its economy to the control of a multinational corporation, and to the robber baron who ran it.[8]

Keith appointed Richard Barthel as the Northern Railroad's new general manager. The 1901 agreement between CAICO and the Guatemalan government stated that Barthel would provide a thousand workers for railroad construction at a government-subsidized salary of fifty cents worth of silver per day.[9] Guatemalan officials provided CAICO with the subsidy to influence the company to abandon its earlier preference for foreign workers in favor of hiring Guatemalan nationals.

In July 1901, Barthel announced to the minister of development that CAICO had "decided to raise the salaries of the ordinary line workers to $1.50 (two reales) [twenty-five cents] a day . . . with the idea of satisfying the workers." To spread the news, he printed 130 flyers and had local officials in several departments post them in strategic locations. At the beginning of August 1901, some 650 men, mostly Guatemalans, surrounded the company's office in Zacapa and, in Barthel's words, all talked "very much in favor of the notices that the authorities of the departments [had] put up."[10]

In the twentieth century, the complex relationship between U.S. corporations and Guatemalan federal and departmental authorities continued. All three continued to collaborate to ensure the availability of unskilled laborers for the completion, maintenance, and expansion of the Northern Railroad. In October 1901, for example, the minister of development ordered government officials in the department of Zacapa to "obtain 150 men for the work of the Northern Railroad."[11] When they could not deliver, railroad officials asked that the minister of development request assistance from officials in the bordering department of Chiquimula in obtaining the workers.[12]

At the turn of the century, the efforts of foreign-born black workers to make the Caribbean coast more hospitable was much more evident than previous efforts, but they were still not enough to attract large numbers of Latin American workers. Over the next fifteen years, black workers, and a slowly increasing number of Latin American workers, would complete the process of modernizing the region and thus making it a far more attractive place to work for locals and Latin Americans from the bordering countries of Honduras and El Salvador. Between the 1880s and 1915, black workers and some Latin Americans finished laying track; built railroad stations, machine shops, and a roundhouse; and cleared the land necessary for the start of United Fruit banana plantations. In addition, company hospitals and very profitable stores were built to meet the commissary demands of blue-collar and white-collar workers. In short, after the essential elements of the railroad infrastructure were in place, the banana boom led to the migration of large numbers of West Indians and Latin Americans to the Caribbean coast of Guatemala.

Interethnic Conflict among Caribbean Coast Workers

The introduction of more workers to the Caribbean coast, particularly black West Indians, made incidents of violent conflict between coastal workers more frequent. A number of variables help to explain the regular reports of fistfights, shootings, and stabbings between coworkers. Frontier conditions, in which men lived in company housing, regularly got drunk, gambled, and suffered periods of economic scarcity and hunger, created a generally rough and violent male culture on the Caribbean coast, which itself had been transformed from a sleepy backwater to an important boom-and-bust banana region—a region with a male-dominated, multiethnic workforce racked with the violent fallout between coworkers rooted in class, race, and national and language differences. Class (and sometimes racial) conflict erupted as one worker robbed another worker who had more money. At other times, racial, linguistic, and national prejudice and rivalries led to violence. John Williams, a former UFCO foreman in Guatemala, had this to say about the conflict between workers: "The negro from the United states has no use for the British subjects. The Jamaican has no regard for the black from Belize or Barbadoes, and still less for the French-speaking negroes and the blacks from the United States." As a result, "numerous fights and small riots" happened in the Guatemalan banana belt.

During the early twentieth century, several violent incidents occurred that were indicative of the multiple rivalries and tensions that existed on the Caribbean coast. On one occasion, for example, white American William Balz, a UFCO hospital steward and manager, pulled a revolver on a Jamaican cook named Collins who was under his supervision. Balz worked at a UFCO hospital in Dartmouth, Guatemala. The trouble began in May 1911 when Balz ordered Collins to stop disturbing the peace. Collins, who was singing loudly on the railing in front of the hospital kitchen, paid no attention to the order. Balz stepped toward the Jamaican cook and sharply repeated his demand for the singing to cease. In a brash tone, Collins asked Balz what he wanted. Seeking to enforce his authority, Balz grabbed Collins by the arm, whereupon the two men began a violent scuffle during which Balz drew his revolver. Balz warned the Jamaican that he would shoot if Collins did not back up, but Collins advanced anyway. Twenty hostile blacks then followed him along a five- or six-mile route to the office of the local authorities. The outcome of the incident is unknown.[13]

As semi-nomadic single men, most Caribbean coast workers in Central America established no real ties to the communities in which they worked for short stints of time. Among this group, threats of violence and the commission of actual violent acts were important ways of asserting masculinity. At times, language barriers caused misunderstandings between English- and Spanish-language speakers. Latin American workers who arrived on the Caribbean coast in search of jobs resented having to compete with English-speaking black workers for employment.[14] African American railroad employee Oscar Bell Payne's account of his repeated armed run-ins with a Guatemalan railroad worker suggests how this resentment sometimes boiled over. Payne had been born in Howard County, Missouri, in 1856. At age twenty-one, he departed the United States to work on the Northern Railroad in Guatemala and other places. Several times, he tried unsuccessfully to return to the United States. In 1895, a Guatemalan coworker stabbed him for no stated reason. Three years later, the same man attacked him on payday with a knife. Again, in 1904, the same man tried to rob Payne of $75 in wages. Payne reported the crime to Guatemalan police officials in Barrios, but instead of arresting the Guatemalan assailant, they arrested Payne and fined him $10. Payne eventually received prison time for killing the Guatemalan man who had robbed him twice.[15]

Four years later, officials in Barrios convicted African American Louis Wilson for murdering a black native of Belize named Lammie. Both black men had worked as waiters at Puerto Barrios's Hotel del Norte. Witnesses said that Wilson went to his room to retrieve his pistol after the two men had engaged in a trivial quarrel. When Wilson returned to the kitchen, he shot Lammie without a word of warning. Guatemalan officials sentenced Wilson to ten years in the penitentiary at Guatemala City. Wilson later died attempting to escape.[16]

Another shooting took place in Puerto Barrios, this time between two black business partners and port police officers named Wilfred Brown and Jorge Morrison. Brown was single and had a high-paying, steady job as an IRCA machinist. Morrison worked as a foremen on UFCO's Virginia banana plantation, a high-paying supervisory job that company officials most often filled with white Americans. Both men had second and third jobs as police officers and co-owners of Hedley Ward's cantina in Puerto Barrios. Brown shot and injured Morrison. The Guatemalan municipal judge of Barrios who presided over the case explained that Brown shot Morrison because Morrison had Brown "arrested for selling liquor after 9:00 p. m. without a license."[17] The speculation here is that Brown and Morrison disagreed over the risk of putting their business and themselves in jeopardy for violating a

Figure 3.1. Laborers loading fruit on a train on the Virginia Plantation in Guatemala

strictly regulated liquor license ordinance, or keeping the cantina open late illegally and earning more profits. The judge added, "It's possible that all involved were Afro-Americans, some from the West Indies some from north america [*sic*]."[18]

In another incident, U.S. citizen James Wilson had a conflict in a bar in Zacapa with a Guatemalan national. After entering the bar, Wilson attempted to walk past the Guatemalan man, who objected, drew his revolver, and aimed it at Wilson. Wilson then snatched the revolver from the Guatemalan and fled the bar. The next day, Zacapa officials arrested Wilson, and later fined him $50 in Guatemalan currency. A contemporary of Wilson's, an expatriate in Zacapa, described the city as a place where "numerous killing affairs [were] common hereabouts."[19]

According to travel writer Eugene Cunningham, "Many full-blooded negroes [Jamaicans, Hondurans, and North Americans] moved among the Guatemalticos and half-breeds" of Zacapa. The writer described "most of" the city's blacks as "well dressed and very pompous in manner."[20] Cunningham visited the combination bar and grocery store of a white American named Charley Swanson in Zacapa. Swanson had been a steamboat cook on the Gulf of Mexico for many years before settling in Zacapa. Cunningham heard Swanson warn a racist Irish American that if he continued to refer to the bar's black customers as "niggers" one of them would suddenly end his life with a "knife between the ribs."[21] Race-based, class-based, and liquor-related conflicts between coworkers of all nationalities could start with a nasty look or racial slur in a bar and quickly spiral into homicide on the largely foreign, male, working-class Caribbean coast.

In May 1912, Morris Brown, an employee of the Northern Railroad, stood trial in a homicide case. Guatemalan authorities had arrested him for shooting a North American coworker named Steward, a conductor on the railroad. Brown was a thirty-one-year-old native of Florida. Before working on the Caribbean coast of Guatemala, he had worked for the Pan American Railroad in Puerto Limón, Costa Rica. In July 1910, he had traveled by steamship from Puerto Limón to Puerto Barrios, where William Penney hired him. The shooting incident took place in a saloon in the town of Morales in the department of Izabal. Steward was one of the proprietors of the saloon. The fight broke out when Brown asked Steward to pay back fifteen dollars he had borrowed a few days earlier. In response to Brown's request, Steward came at Brown with a dagger. In his defense, Brown fired two shots at Steward; the second shot hit Steward in the chest, wounding him seriously but not killing him.[22]

Such small-scale disputes could quickly escalate to involve multiple Guatemalan residents. One such riot occurred on the UFCO's Tehuana plantation in May 1914. Jamaican laborer Alfred Esson was shooting dice with some Guatemalan and Honduran laborers. Using either skill or loaded dice, Esson parted the laborers from their money. Owen H. Hughes, a twenty-six-year-old unmarried North American foreman and resident of the farm, witnessed a mob of forty-five Guatemalan and Honduran men chasing, overtaking, and killing Esson shortly thereafter.[23] The next day, a mob of Jamaicans brandishing revolvers and machetes gathered to avenge the death of their countryman. They raided the Guatemalan section of the company housing and killed and injured several Guatemalans.[24] When the Guatemalan authority received news of the disorder, he immediately telegraphed President Estrada Cabrera, informing him that sixty armed blacks had slayed a number of Guatemalan nationals and injured others.[25] The president requested that local officials in Izabal send him a detailed description of the disturbance and a list of steps necessary to stop the rioting and to jail the blacks involved.[26]

As a general policy, Estrada Cabrera handpicked the governors, mayors, and municipal judges installed throughout provincial Guatemala. In addition, he placed armed national troops at strategic locations in each department to back the local governments that supported his regime. National military garrisons around the country and the use of the telegraph allowed him to influence the body politic at the local and national levels. This was true because local officials depended on national troops to keep public order. His control of the military allowed Estrada Cabrera to almost independently determine public policy.[27]

During the May 1914 race riot—one of the many examples of social unrest on the Caribbean coast involving black workers—Estrada Cabrera called for a coordinated effort and mutual assistance from the *jefes políticos* and *comandantes* of arms throughout the region. He demanded the utmost care in preventing future race riots on the coast.[28] One local official on the scene called for additional troops, which national officials quickly dispatched from surrounding garrisons in Livingston, Gualán, and Zacapa. The soldiers divided into three squads and took separate routes into the trouble spots on two banana plantations. After two days, the soldiers had killed and wounded several Jamaicans and confined several others to the Zacapa jail. After many other workers fled in terror from their barracks, the soldiers and their commanding officers robbed their quarters and destroyed their personal property. During the plunder of the barracks, they killed, wounded, and jailed additional Jamaicans. The military operation scattered laborers for a day or so and practically shut down the Quiché and Tehuana banana plantations. On May 17, a commandant and twenty-six soldiers remained on guard at a nearby railway station because state officials feared that armed Jamaicans from surrounding areas would go to Zacapa to rescue their captured countrymen. Additional soldiers in Zacapa guarded the Jamaican prisoners in the municipal jail. Department officials eventually convicted the Jamaicans of the murder of the four Guatemalans and of disrupting public order on the UFCO plantations. Peace and quiet did return to the Caribbean coast, but at the cost of many lives, injuries, and the incarceration of black immigrant laborers.[29]

The testimony about the Tehuana riot by Guatemalan Carmen Villagrán reveals that a railroad track divided the Jamaicans' company housing from the residences of UFCO's Honduran and Guatemalan laborers on the Tehuana plantation. The thirty-year-old Villagrán, who was married, literate, and employed as a domestic on the plantation, stated that when the row broke out, the Jamaicans crossed the tracks, killing two Guatemalan men and injuring others; the rest of the Guatemalan men escaped by running off. The Jamaicans then turned to attack the Guatemalan women on the plantation, but, according to Villagrán, they stopped when three African Americans came to the women's aid. The African Americans persuaded the Jamaican mob not to harm the innocent women. Twenty-nine-year-old Guatemalan Rita Flores, who lived on the Tehuana plantation, confirmed that many of the Guatemalans dispersed in various directions, with several Jamaicans in pursuit. In search of safety, the women crossed the railroad tracks and took refuge among the African Americans, who defended them.[30]

In contrast to the safety Guatemalan women felt among the African Americans, Villagrán viewed Jamaican men as dangerous and threatening individuals who regularly committed "all class of offenses against" Latin Americans. According to her affidavit, gangs of Jamaican men went around assaulting and killing Guatemalan men and women without any remorse. She expressed the opinion that Jamaicans had it in for Latin Americans.[31] According to one eyewitness, the riot unleashed hatred and mistrust between workers of different races and nationalities on the plantation.

The arrival of the national troops increased the violence and tensions that already existed between black and Latin American coworkers on the Caribbean coast.[32] George Ferguson, a member of the UFCO security force, testified that the Sunday following the start of the conflict, the Jamaicans on the farms set out drunk and armed with "pistols and machetes" to avenge "their dead countrymen" by killing has many Latin Americans as they could find without any mercy.[33] In a Guatemalan police report, a Guatemalan laborer on the Tehuana plantation provided similar descriptions of the Jamaican workers. He reported seeing large numbers of them between Tehuana and a nearby railroad labor camp attacking a group of Guatemalans and Hondurans with pistols. The Jamaicans then boarded a train, threw several Latin American men from a passenger car, and kept a number of women for their own designs.[34]

What these diverse incidents of interethnic violence suggest is not so much endemic conflict as an environment in which most of the criminal activity of immigrant workers, which often involved the use of guns and knives, was rooted in cultural and linguistic differences and excessive drinking and gambling by both black and Latin American workers. In this somewhat wild border context, however, not all workers were treated equally: Guatemalan officials assigned stiffer fines and jail sentences to the black participants in criminal activities than they did to Guatemalan nationals. When in trouble with local officials, moreover, working-class black U.S. nationals who were Republicans did not receive much in the way of assistance from the white Democrats serving as U.S. consular agents.

Anti-Immigrant Sentiments in Guatemala

Following the riot, Estrada Cabrera issued an executive decree in 1914 which required immigrants of color to deposit fifty dollars in gold at the customs house of their port of entry, to be returned to them upon their departure from the country.[35] Some argue that the president passed the law to stop the entrance of black laborers, and the subsequent Africanization of Guatemala's Caribbean coast. Above all, racist government ministers wanted white immigrants who could positively influence Guatemala's largely Mayan population.[36]

American consul Stuart Lipton described Guatemala's immigration policy as liberal but written to prohibit the entrance of non-white immigrants. Despite this policy, Guatemala had a sizable Chinese expatriate community, whose earliest members had arrived as contract laborers. Many of them had settled permanently in Guatemala despite daily encounters with Guatemalan nationalism and racism. The Chinese worked as merchants in small stores in almost every banana plantation town on the coast, and in other regions of Guatemala as well. Despite their success, restrictions on Chinese and African American immigrants continued. After 1914, the government of Guatemala began closely monitoring the movement of immigrants of Chinese and African descent. Thereafter, only those who could afford the mandatory fifty dollar deposit at the customs office entered the country.

One of the few who could afford the deposit was Rafael Fong. Born in Canton, China, Fong worked as merchant in the municipality of Morales, Izabal. Guatemala census records tell us that Morales had a population of 475 people in 1893 and no banana plantations. By 1921, the municipality had a population of 3,564 people and thirty banana plantations; 2,454 people lived on the plantations. Fong was unmarried and had two children living with him in Morales: two-year-old Luz and four-year-old Rafael.[37]

Anti-immigrant sentiment in Guatemala continued to be strong into the 1920s. On one occasion, U.S. officials felt compelled to intervene on the side of the Chinese expatriate community during a period of intense anti-Chinese feeling. In 1920, Herbert S. Gold wrote the Guatemalan minister of foreign affairs that the North American legation "sincerely hoped" that the president of Guatemala would issue an executive decree demanding the immediate end of all propaganda and of "the campaign against citizens of the Chinese Republic residing in [Guatemala]." Guatemalan citizens, according to Gold, had started a brutal anti-Chinese campaign. He added that a new nativist periodical called *La Vida Nueva* had published inflammatory articles about the country's Chinese diaspora. In addition, a nativist organization called the

Liga Patriótica had held a meeting where speakers slandered the Chinese.[38] In the fall of 1921, the president of Guatemala modified the October 1914 policy that required immigrants of color to make a deposit of fifty dollars. The new executive decree required immigrants of color to deposit two hundred pesos in American gold with customs officials before disembarking at any Guatemalan port.[39] The immediate cause of the anti-Chinese movement in Guatemala is unknown. In Costa Rica, however, similar movements and attitudes developed out of racist myths that claimed Chinese immigrants spread venereal disease and promoted sex-related criminal activity.[40]

White foreigners interested in entering the country were treated quite differently. Because they were desired citizens, the government offered whites an open-door policy, free transportation to Guatemala, and land on which to settle.[41] In the summer of 1921, the Guatemalan government organized its new Foreign Service and Publicity Bureau. The new agency published a brochure with a description of Guatemala and other useful information to attract white immigrants. The advertisement clearly stated that Africans and Asians would not receive authorization to enter the country but that Guatemala offered excellent opportunities for ambitious white immigrants who were willing to work.[42]

Beginning at the turn of the twentieth century, when Minor Keith's company won a government contract that enabled UFCO's influence to expand into the Guatemalan interior, the composition of the UFCO and IRCA workforce began to shift, comprising increasingly larger numbers of Latin Americans and fewer Caribbean blacks and African Americans. This shift was the result of deliberate Guatemalan government policy, as well as the natural result of workers' movement into other occupations. Interethnic tensions simmered below the surface in this workforce made up of uprooted men of different races, languages, and national allegiances, and these tensions were exacerbated and highlighted by local officials' mistreatment of foreign-born workers as well as anti-immigration government policies. As the next chapter will show, however, to focus solely on interethnic conflict among the coastal labor force is to miss the point, as workers collaborated on several occasions in the first two decades of the twentieth century to improve their common lot.

4

Revolvers, Shotguns, Machetes, and Clubs

The Strikes of 1909–1919

On December 7, 1909, Warren W. Smith, the superintendent of the various farms of the United Fruit Company, described the start of a banana plantation labor strike that quickly spread across the department of Izabal. One morning, while riding through the Virginia plantation, he met "a mob of strikers armed with revolvers, shot-guns, machetes, and clubs," who told him that they were going to flog a Jamaican on the plantation who had refused to support a collective work stoppage. In addition, when a train loaded with freshly cut bananas was ready to depart the plantation, the strikers forcefully removed railroad workers from the train. Smith called on the local comandante to maintain order, but the strikers disregarded the soldiers' show of force, and the train never made it off the plantation. The strikers then moved on to another plantation to forcefully drive Jamaican, Guatemalan, and North American strikebreakers off the job.[1]

The strikers declared that so long as their demands for increased pay remained unsatisfied, "all laborers, regardless of nationality would be driven off the farms." They then sent notices around to other plantations, threatening harm to all strikebreakers. Each day, they became increasingly more militant, promising to shoot the first man who attempted to load a freight train with fruit. Armed strikers even entered into a shootout with some white UFCO employees whom they encountered while seizing one of the company banana trains.[2]

It is difficult to square descriptions of Guatemalan labor militancy such as this one with the long-standing picture of UFCO and IRCA workers as being thoroughly subordinate to their employers and divided among themselves—a stereotype that the previous chapter reinforces. A 1936 social history of the banana industry describes worker mobilization efforts during the administration of dictator Estrada Cabrera as impotent, and strikes as virtually impossible under autocratic military rule. This interpretation insists that the army in Guatemala quickly moved to crush UFCO and IRCA labor strikes.

Figure 4.1. Loading bananas in United Fruit's Guatemalan Division

Similarly, a study of banana workers in Panama reveals that workers there suffered from "the twin blows of economic hardship and repressive political rule."[3] Some scholars have argued that UFCO and its managers in Guatemala reinforced and manipulated race and class distinctions to undermine and limit worker mobilization efforts. According to this interpretation, the company capitalized on highly emotional, inbred racism rooted in job competition and cultural differences between laborers of African descent and Latin Americans.[4]

A contrasting depiction of labor solidarity in studies of Guatemala and Costa Rica by Stephen Gillick and Ron Harpelle, however, acknowledges that while UFCO managers encouraged ethnic rivalries between black and Latin American workers, workers united over the need for higher wages.[5] Likewise, this chapter acknowledges that UFCO managers and the dictator Estrada Cabrera made working-class mobilization efforts challenging in Guatemala. Accounts of worker mobilization efforts between 1909 and 1915, however, provide a compelling argument against the popular view of labor as having been passive during the Estrada Cabrera dictatorship. Workers were not always divided, impotent, or incapable of confronting company and state officials.[6] I argue that the laborers' common struggle against racist white employers helped to obscure ethnic, linguistic, cultural, religious, and national differences among them and sometimes allowed for the mobilization of large groups of strikers.[7]

The Color Line as a Unifying Force

With so many black immigrants the Guatemalan Caribbean coast developed an African diaspora made up of black foreigners and native Garifuna. As we have seen, intra-diaspora conflicts did occur, but diverse black and Latin American employees also united against their white employers.

Guatemalan nationals and foreign-born black workers quickly closed ranks when it came to facing challenges from white company officials.[8] Trouble resulted when racist white bosses tried to enforce a rigid Jim Crow policy in which people of color had to show deference to whites. The deference policy required non-white workers to yield to whites on walkways and to take off their hats when talking to whites. White bosses also prohibited black and Latin American laborers from entering the front yards of their residences. Such policies proved difficult to enforce, however, because Jamaican workers, as British subjects, believed they were equal to, if not better than, non-British subjects. Both Latin Americans and workers of African descent fiercely fought the attempts of racist white bosses to maintain separate and unequal Jim Crow conditions in employment, food, housing, living conditions, and recreational facilities.[9]

As a result of the color line, blacks and whites perpetrated violence against each other, which often resulted in serious injury or death. At times, white bosses depended on African American collaborators to spy on laborers and tip them off about the militant actions of Jamaican workers. White bosses also hired hit men to kill black workers for as little as ten dollars in U.S. gold. The political assassination of belligerent blacks on the Caribbean coast occurred regularly and discreetly: "the body slipped into the river where the alligators removed all evidence of the crime."[10] One Jamaican, who murdered a white railroad contractor, escaped to Honduras. Had he been captured by white coastal residents, his fate would have been very different: they would most likely have lynched him or run a locomotive over him, as had happened to others before him. Instead, a bribe paid in gold to a *comandante* in Honduras ensured the extradition of the accused to authorities in Guatemala. The majority of both Latin American workers and workers of African descent on the coast understood that white UFCO employers viewed them with contempt, and this, as well as their often wretched working conditions, gave them a common enemy.[11]

The 1909 Banana Strike

In December 1909 some laborers on the Cayuga and Virginia UFCO banana plantations went on strike to demand higher wages and better treatment from their overseer. Despite the workers' complaints about his behavior, the overseer refused to make any changes or adjustments. In response, the workers requested that company officials replace the overseer with a more agreeable person. UFCO officials accused Jamaicans George Archer, Daniel Lindsay, and Robert Anderson of being the principal leaders and organizers of the strike. According to Godfrey Haggard, a Jamaican member of the UFCO security force, the three organizers of the strike were not company employees. Therefore, he said, "they don't have the right to be here,—much less to involve themselves in this ordeal." This statement seems to imply that Archer, Lindsay, and Anderson came to Izabal specifically to organize laborers.[12] The three Jamaicans used the banana trains on the Northern Railroad to send a message out to UFCO workers from an organization they called the Jamaica Union. The message informed readers that the strike organizers would hold a meeting the following day on the Tenedores plantation. At the meeting, they would discuss organizing a general strike across UFCO's Guatemalan division. The note read, "Remember boys we are all Jamaicans."[13] While such an appeal to nationality probably helped the organizers forge a connection between striking workers, the Jamaican workers also faced the challenge of convincing African American and Latin American workers to join in a united front against UFCO managers.

UFCO company correspondence shows that the leaders of the Jamaica Union mobilized some four hundred laborers. These workers were primarily Jamaican, but a few were African Americans. Some African American laborers were swayed to join the Jamaica Union because they identified with the collective negative experience of working for racist UFCO officials. Others most likely sought to increase their pay and improve their working conditions. As we have seen, still others had to be physically forced to capitulate by union members armed with revolvers, shotguns, machetes, and clubs. As the strike moved to other sections of the plantation region, some workers freely joined the union, while others resisted. The strikers flogged and removed one Jamaican laborer who refused to stop cutting bananas and support the walkout from a field.[14]

The 1909 strikers hijacked a fruit train packed with bananas and "forcefully removed all the men off the train." In Cayuga, the strikers apparently derailed a railroad car and promised to shoot the first man who attempted to load a fruit train with bananas. The move ensured that no bananas would reach Puerto Barrios and that UFCO would not be able to ship bananas to profitable markets in the United States. A group of striking workers from the Virginia plantation traveled to Seneca Farm, where they forced Jamaicans, Latin Americans, and North Americans out of the fields. They declared that so long as their demands for increased pay remained unsatisfied, "all laborers, regardless of nationality would be driven off the farms."[15]

After the strike began, organizers published their demands and distributed them to UFCO workers throughout the Caribbean coast region. In one instance, a frightened white UFCO supervisor with a revolver started shooting wildly at a group of workers. The workers immediately returned his fire. The situation intensified after the white official wounded one of the strikers. Black strikers then fired at some white men on top of a nearby train car who had taken no part in the shooting. Some black strikers headed to Barrios in pursuit of the gunman, promising to "take the life of any white man they met."[16]

Guatemalan soldiers arrested two of the strikers at the Cayuga plantation for plundering the UFCO commissary there. A detachment of the striking workers then threatened to "destroy the comandancia" if Guatemalan officials did not release members of their group. A UFCO official ordered the men released, "knowing that if the men started a riot that the soldiers being so few in number would not be able to control the situation." Shortly thereafter, the strikers moved onto the Dartmouth plantation, where they ransacked another UFCO commissary. Company officials estimated the total loss "at about $5000.00 gold."[17]

United Fruit Company Wraps Itself in the American Flag

In its confrontation with the striking workers, UFCO turned for protection to its own security forces and to its status as a wealthy North American corporation. On numerous occasions, company officials requested that the U.S. State Department use its diplomatic channels to get the Guatemalan government to help UFCO confront the strikers. At the beginning of the strike, UFCO superintendent Warren W. Smith telegraphed William F. Sands of the American legation to Guatemala from his office in Puerto Barrios. He asked Sands to solicit high-ranking Guatemalan officials to dispatch soldiers by train to all the farms that night, as the situation had become "serious." Guatemalan officials met the request for soldiers.[18]

UFCO's Victor M. Cutter was much more specific. He requested that Guatemalan officials in the capital dispatch one hundred soldiers to Virginia, twenty-five to Dartmouth, and fifty to the Cayuga plantation. In addition, Smith later telegraphed Nicolas Ferguson, UFCO's *comandante* on the Virginia plantation, to "please arrest and put in prison" several members of the Jamaican Union for "robbing the commissaries, invading the plantations, carry[ing] firing arms, and mistreating people." At the local level, Smith called on Consular Agent Reed in Izabal to assist him by communicating with the department's governor and military commander.[19] On the same day, Reed wrote the governor asking him to arrest African American and Jamaican UFCO laborers involved in the strike. "In addition I ask that you proceed to disarm all individuals carrying arms illegally," Reed wrote.[20] But despite his pleadings, at the end of December 1909 the Jamaican Union strike still had momentum. The poor placement of Guatemalan soldiers on the various plantations and the sustained efforts of the strike leaders accounted for the strike's persistence.

Jamaican police officer Godfrey Haggard reported to the governor of Izabal that, thanks to the presence of the soldiers, "some of the men [had] returned to work and the majority of the Jamaicans" had decided to end the work stoppage and organized protest. In Haggard's opinion, removing Archer, Lindsay, and Anderson would be a sure way "to get rid of this rebellious element among the men."[21] Yet two days after Haggard's report, Guatemalan officials had still done nothing to arrest the leaders of the strike or to disarm the workers who supported it.[22] At the beginning of January 1910, Smith reported, "The strikers are still active, and the local authorities are not sufficient to impede whatever movement they will plan." Instead of strengthening their efforts, Guatemalan officials withdrew soldiers from the Virginia plantation. This concerned Smith. Company officials had already scheduled a banana harvesting and shipping day for the first week in January. The next day, too, Guatemalan officials did nothing to apprehend the British subjects assumed to be the leaders of the strike or to calm "the rebellious element among the men." Smith went so far as to meet with a judge who had jurisdiction over the region to discuss his concerns, but still the strike leaders remained at large.[23]

Smith compromised in his next request to the governor of Izabal, advising the governor to withdraw troops in detachments of fifteen, as the timing seemed appropriate. But after Smith had sent Izabal governor Luis Estrada Monzón three messages to that effect, the governor notified Smith that he planned to withdraw the troops all at once, which Smith believed would encourage the strikers to continue their work stoppage. Smith wrote of his infuriation with the departmental officials responsible for initiating the withdrawal: the company had made "every effort" to keep the soldiers satisfied, he said, including providing medical care, "provisions and wages to the entire force" during the period of its occupation.[24] Why was the Guatemalan government so reluctant to take action to secure the company's interests?

The Limits of Estrada Cabrera's Domination

Why could not dictator Estrada Cabrera entirely repress the mobilization efforts of the striking workers? A letter from Hugh R. Wilson, the American chargé d'affaires to the U.S. secretary of state, provides a partial answer. Wilson explains that Estrada Cabrera would not take military action against the striking workers because the majority of them were Jamaicans. The British foreign minister to Guatemala had informed Estrada Cabrera that he would be held "responsible for the lives of all British subjects lost in the disturbance."[25] According to William Sands, the stance of the British ministers in Guatemala City "made the authorities over cautious in dealing with the rioters." Between the U.S. and British legations, President Estrada Cabrera "was in a delicate position, and wished to simply drive the rioters out of the country, arbitrarily, with out making any arrests." This policy called for ousting the strike organizers from Guatemala until interest in their arrest subsided.[26]

In February 1910, UFCO manager Victor Cutter reported: "The handful of men who went away after the robbing of the Company's store have now returned, since they find that no punishment was likely to be enforced upon them." U.S. officials wanted local authorities in Izabal to prosecute the strikers to the full extent of Guatemalan law. Estrada Cabrera refused to send any such orders to officials on the Caribbean coast, however, because he could not afford to antagonize the British foreign minister.[27] Since the end of the colonial period, the British had exercised considerable neocolonial power in Guatemala; Britain had over $40 million invested in the republic. Because of this, Estrada Cabrera instructed his minister of government and justice to ensure that local officials used restraint instead of reckless force, and to impede the characterization of Jamaicans as dangerous criminals.[28]

Thereafter, officials in Izabal proceeded slowly and cautiously in their investigation into cases involving British subjects accused of violating Guatemalan laws during the strike. In a March 1910 letter to Cutter, Lionel Carden of the British legation to Guatemala defended his country's diplomatic position. "I have not the smallest sympathy with rioters or lawbreakers," said Carden. "All I ask, if they are British subjects, is that they be fairly tried in accordance with the laws and given proper facilities for defending themselves. If convicted, by all means let them be punished."[29]

U.S. and UFCO officials also clashed with the British legation over the right of banana workers to bear arms. On several occasions after the start of the strike, U.S. diplomats and company officials requested the governor of the department of Izabal to disarm the laborers, and especially "all individuals carrying arms illegally."[30] The British minister responded to company officials that, according to Guatemalan laws, "neither natives nor foreigners are allowed to carry arms on their persons without a written permit from the proper authority." Thus, the legation had no intention of protecting British subjects who broke this law. Except when a crime had been committed, however, the legation would protect those who legally possessed arms in their homes for self-defense, and it would not tolerate government officials who searched "a man's house merely to see if he had arms, or to confiscate them if he found them." Cutter responded to Carden's remarks by saying that UFCO would fire "at once any man carrying arms" but would not get involved "with disarming men who carry arms illegally." In such cases, the company expected local Guatemalan officials to prosecute the offenders.[31]

Continued pressure on the U.S. government from UFCO officials produced some results. U.S. officials forced the Guatemalan government to take more than token steps toward maintaining order on the Caribbean coast. This led to the capture of two of the strike leaders.[32] Izabal officials had also begun to champion the "suppression of illegal liquor sales," Cutter noted, and, consequently, "conditions on the coast" improved.[33] By April 1910, Izabal officials had captured and prosecuted all three of the strike leaders. In August, a high court of Guatemala sentenced the three, plus two others, to serve five years and four months each in the Central Penitentiary in Guatemala City, located far from the Caribbean coast.[34]

In the final analysis, then, the Guatemalan military repressed the strike. The length of time it took, however, undermined the government's credibility in the eyes of coastal laborers. Moreover, the ability of the striking workers to outnumber soldiers and to successfully demand the release of their colleagues from the Cayuga *comandancia* must have struck fear into the hearts of Caribbean coast officials and their subordinates. At times, striking workers had white UFCO officials and Guatemalan soldiers on the run and seeking cover. According to one Caribbean coast resident, the black workers did not fear the company.[35]

In order to regain control of public order in the region, officials in Izabal suggested establishing "a force of soldiers on the plantations," to be paid for by the company. UFCO preferred to maintain its own small police force comprised of members selected by local government officials; it had developed and used this approach successfully in its Costa Rica division. In August 1913, Cutter and Luis Estrada Monzón, the governor of Izabal, discussed the four candidates under consideration for two recently created UFCO police agent positions on the Caribbean coast. Each agent would receive a monthly UFCO salary of twenty-five pesos in U.S. gold, in addition to company housing. Cutter wanted to hire at least one Jamaican agent who was fluent in Spanish.[36]

The arrival of Guatemalan soldiers and the swift arrest and imprisonment of union leaders ended the strike. Furthermore, UFCO's decision to militarize the banana enclave, arrest suspected strike leaders, and disarm workers was an important factor in temporarily reducing the union's strength. There is no indication in the archival record that striking workers won any of their demands from UFCO officials before returning to work in August 1910.

The 1913 Railroad Strike

In the spring of 1913, a multiethnic group of brakemen on IRCA's Central Railroad line in the Pacific coast department of Escuintla went on strike for increased wages, job security, and the legal right to strike. F. G. Williamson, IRCA's superintendent in Guatemala, received a telegram announcing that some of the Puerto Barrios firemen had simultaneously gone on strike.[37] The small but outspoken militant group of strikers used fear to successfully prevent the majority of their coworkers from crossing the picket line. An IRCA official in charge at Escuintla sent Williamson a telegram that said that none of his men were working that day. He explained: "The whole work gang is situated at the gate, armed with rocks."[38]

The strikers had leverage to use against the company because much of the republic depended on railroad transportation for the delivery of cattle to local slaughterhouses. The first consequence of the strike for Guatemalans, therefore, would be a meat shortage.[39] Public demand for meat and for the return of the regular movement of trains and the mail worked to force a speedy IRCA acceptance of the strikers' demands. IRCA officials and the workers did not reach "a definitive arrangement" right away, but they made enough progress for the striking workers to return to their jobs on April 5, 1913.[40]

While the strike was still going on, Puerto Barrios authorities arrested fifteen strikers suspected of harassing replacement workers. IRCA's hardline stance caused more problems than it solved. In April 1913, "close to 40 strikers" from Puerto Barrios marched to the company's Zacapa offices in protest of the arrests. Someone informed Williamson that President Estrada Cabrera had ordered the men to converge on Zacapa to receive their pay;

however, there is no evidence that this was the case, nor is there evidence about who started the rumor. In response to the presence of the hostile laborers, Williamson lobbied the governor of Zacapa for military protection for company property and personnel. The militant, multiethnic group of striking workers evidently frightened the generally bold and arrogant Williamson, at least for the moment. But the arrival of government troops provided him with a brief break; the following day, the laborers ended their strike.[41]

Worker militancy paid off for the strikers, who from the beginning wanted increases that would allow them to meet their expenses. Williamson gave all IRCA employees, both workers who had gone on strike and those who had stayed on the job, pay increases ranging from 10 percent to 25 percent. He apparently authorized the wage increases to stop the spread of the strike to other areas of the railroad workforce. At the same time, he made it clear to the returning workers that the company reserved the "right to employ numerically only those it wants to keep in its service," and that it would not be compelled to hire again workers who were "not worth the wages that they [were] being paid."[42] This last stipulation on Williamson's part shortly caused another strike. Confidential negotiations took place between the strikers and Williamson, with the two sides finally hammering out a tenuous agreement. Williamson received news that the strikers had ended their walkout, but he did not believe it would be long before another strike would happen.[43]

Members of IRCA's multiethnic, militant workforce were becoming increasingly aware of the power of collective action as a proven strategy for achieving wage increases. In an attempt to repress union organizing and strikes, Williamson discharged several outspoken members of the workforce. In response to the discharge of their coworkers, some IRCA laborers made comments openly attacking Williamson. These comments were later published in the Guatemalan press. The situation seemed so alarming to U.S. officials that they requested that Guatemalan officials take steps to repress future inflammatory pronouncements and to provide for Williamson's personal security.[44]

The 1915 Waterfront Strike

On January 16, 1915, dockworkers at Puerto Barrios went on strike because they wanted an increase in the daily pay they received for five to six hours of hauling banana bunches.[45] The striking laborers obtained indirect assistance from the governor of Izabal, who told UFCO officials that he believed that the men should receive $1.50 per day. Local authorities further undermined UFCO's position by refusing to provide police protection for the replacement workers or company property.[46]

According Joaquin Hecht, the acting consular agent at Puerto Barrios, "If the authorities had taken a firm stand, the whole matter would have been settled at once, but as it was, the strikers believed they had government protection and prevented the men who were willing to work from going on the wharf." The workers clearly saw that that the governor was reluctant to support the foreign company, and, as a result, they took bold steps. In addition to threatening the men who volunteered to work, striking workers "tried to derail one of the banana trains." When the strike dragged on for almost a week, UFCO officials used high-ranking U.S. diplomatic channels to get President Estrada Cabrera to obtain cooperation from local authorities at Puerto Barrios.[47]

Toward the end of January 1915, UFCO officials went to see the Guatemalan president in his government palace in Guatemala City. He agreed to ensure that the workers would receive no more than $1.25 per day for 10 hours' work, and he promised to deport the strike leaders. Local officials continued to remain impartial during the strike, however, refusing to enforce the deal or to carry out the order to expel the leaders of the strike. "In my opinion," wrote Hecht, "these local officials are afraid that the strikers will do them personal harm, and besides, they don't want the Co[mpany] to gain its point."[48]

On their own, IRCA officials captured striking workers who tried to derail a train. Yet despite the testimony of eyewitnesses who placed these workers at the scene of the crime, local officials set them free, "at the request of the strikers." Hecht wrote: "If the strikers would have had the intention of killing off every white man and destroy[ing] the property of foreign companies, they could have done so with impunity, as the authorities would not have turned a hand." He added, "In all probability the authorities would have taken to the woods." In the absence of "diplomatic intervention" or pressure from Estrada Cabrera, he thought, local officials in Izabal would continue their "inutility" in repressing the dockworkers' strike.[49] The strike finally ended on or about January 22 with UFCO officially and reluctantly agreeing to the workers' demands for an increase in their banana-stems hauling fee and in their hourly wages. After the strikers received notice of these terms, local authorities in Barrios finally responded to the repeated telegraphs from President Estrada Cabrera ordering them to provide protection for UFCO officials and property and to deport the strike leaders, although in the latter case, probably nothing was done.[50]

We can only speculate about why relations between black UFCO workers and local authorities improved in Puerto Barrios. It is possible that black officers hired by the Guatemalan government after 1913 were responsible for the improvement in relations, helping to delay local authorities' implementation of presidential orders to crack down on striking coastal workers. Certainly, black police officers had extremely close immigration, race, class, and national affinities with plantation, railroad, and dockworkers, with whom they may have roomed, ate, drank, and gambled at one time or the other. We know, for example, that by 1913 UFCO and officials in the Guatemalan Ministry of Government were submitting the names of "honorable individuals" to be selected by the *jefe politico* of Izabal as "police agents." Its not clear if these were people hired as informants or as peace officers. Victor M. Cutter, the manager of UFCO Guatemala, wrote that he thought it would be "convenient" if some of the new agents were given posts on UFCO plantations, and "in addition if one [could] be a Jamaican that knows Spanish."[51] By September 1913, two black officers, that we know of, were identified by a municipal judge of Puerto Barrios as "urban police agents of Puerto Barrios."[52] Puerto Barrios police agent Jorge Morrison, moreover, had once been a UFCO foreman on the Virginia plantation in Morales. One wonders whether Morrison had become so acculturated that he Hispanicized his first name, or whether Morrison's English-speaking friends who worked on the docks, railroad, and plantations called him George while his Spanish-speaking coworkers on the police force called him Jorge.[53]

The 1918 Railroad Strike

Three years after the dockworkers went on strike, Izabal authorities continued to exhibit sympathy with—or fear toward—Caribbean coast workers, and contempt for foreign-owned companies. In December 1918, IRCA and UFCO workers at Puerto Barrios went on strike because the cost of living had doubled on the Caribbean coast since the start of World War I and company officials refused to provide cost-of-living adjustments for their work force. In other regions of the Central American Caribbean world, laborers also organized strikes in December 1918. A British report on the cause of a Jamaican-led UFCO strike in Bocas del Toro, Panama, illustrates the relationship between international developments during World War I and conditions at the local level in Central America:

There are some 4,000 or 5,000 labourers employed on the plantations, practically all of whom are British West Indians, the superintendents being white Americans. . . . Prior to the war, these labourers were comparatively well paid and could live comfortably in their own way, most of them being able to save money with a view to returning ultimately to their native islands to settle there. With the outbreak of war, however, the cost of living began to increase, while their earnings remained the same; and when the United States entered the war a number of ships belonging to the [United Fruit] company were requisitioned by the Government and taken off the Bocas run, with the result that work in the district became less regular and wages went down. Meanwhile, prices of foodstuffs and other necessaries continued to soar and the position of the labourers became gradually worse. While the war lasted they bore with their lot and no actual trouble occurred; but when the armistice came they expected that food prices would automatically fall and that there would be an immediate increase in work and wages; instead of which there was for a time no appreciable effect. As a result they became more and more discontented, and their dissatisfaction culminated in December 1918 in a general strike, which lasted several weeks and gave rise to some ugly incidents. The labourers were not organized, however, and there was no trade union of any kind in the district. The strikers were ultimately prevailed upon to return to work on the understanding that their grievances would be enquired into. A certain amount of discontent, however, which is being fomented by outsiders in the district, who are believed to have been largely responsible for the original strike, continued to exist.[54]

In Izabal and Zacapa, African American workers—West Indians, U.S. blacks, and Central American Garifuna—had instigated all the previous strikes, and Guatemalan and other Latin American workers generally respected them. In contrast to the earlier struggles with IRCA and UFCO, however, it was Guatemalan nationals who started the 1918 strike, and African American workers who followed suit or suffered retribution.[55]

In a December 2, 1918, letter to Jack Armstrong of the British legation in Guatemala City, U.S. consular agent Edward Reed wrote, "When the governor of Izabal and I arrived at Puerto Barrios we found that the strike was brought about by the natives and was being managed by them, there is no doubt but what the Jamaicans and Caribs sympathized." He added: "I spoke to several groups of Jamaicans and they all said that they were willing to work, but that the natives had informed them, that they would not prevent them from working, but at night they would get evan [sic] with them for going to work, so when the whistle sounded for them to 'to turn to' they did not put in an appearance, notwithstanding this statement the crowd of men standing about was made up indiscriminately of natives, Jamaicans, and Caribs."[56]

At the time of the 1918 strike, rumors of an emerging revolutionary movement to overthrow the Estrada Cabrera government flourished. Anonymous members of the revolutionary vanguard met secretly with Walter C. Thurston of the American legation to Guatemala. They warned Thurston that if the United States did not do something to "remedy the situation," members of the opposition movement would. Economic conditions favored both the railroad strike and political instability, as the nation's exchange rate of thirty pesos to the dollar caused a financial depression in the fall of 1918. Some believed that "President [Estrada] Cabrera secretly encouraged the strikers and openly opposed them."[57]

As in Bocas del Toro, Panama, Guatemalan officials believed that radical outsiders, possibly connected with the Mexican Revolution, had fueled worker discontent. Guatemalan newspapers, on the other hand, blamed laborers of African descent. Either way, President Estrada Cabrera quickly dispatched Guatemalan military personnel to protect IRCA and UFCO property and end the strike. According to Thurston, the trouble started up again at the end of January 1919, over the "dismissal of several American engineers." By February, the strike had heated up, when, as Thurston put it, "a small number [of] Guatemalan IRCA fireman requested more pay which was not immediately granted." The strike ended in mid-February without violence or damage to IRCA property.

Analysis of the mobilization of UFCO and IRCA workers in the first two decades of the twentieth century reveals the extent to which the common scholarly emphasis on divisions among this workforce misses an important point: the same workers who were often at one another's throats in barroom brawls and boardinghouse fights also united against their employers on several occasions in an effort to secure better conditions. That these efforts were mostly futile, in the face of the company's influence over the Guatemalan state, should not obscure either the importance of the workers' solidarity or the successes they achieved when they were able to leverage the tension between U.S. and British influence on the Guatemalan government or those governments' control over the railroads to their advantage. As the next chapter reveals, moreover, Estrada Cabrera's government had not completely escaped political instability resulting from domestic unrest and foreign manipulation. A revolution in 1920, which Guatemalans workers on the Caribbean coast supported, soon signaled the end of his long dictatorship.

5

Labor Radicalism on the Caribbean Coast

Ladino Mobilization in Guatemala, 1920–1923

Following the First World War, relations among workers on the Caribbean coast of Guatemala entered a new phase, in which Latin American and black laborers mobilized separately and pursued distinctly different strategies to secure better conditions. This was due in part to the shifting composition of the coastal workforce, which increasingly encompassed a greater number of Latin American laborers and fewer newly arriving migrants. But it was also due to the ways in which Guatemalan labor politics of the post–World War I period drew on regional and international labor movements to foster militancy, anti-imperialism, and nationalism, encouraging the mobilization of Latin American workers at the same time that it pitted them against black migrants and their North American employers. This chapter explores the mobilization of Latin American workers in the early 1920s, when a revolution overturned the status quo and opened a space for labor militancy that was realized in major strikes of railroad and dockworkers, the latter of which threatened to upset the regime for a second time.

The Guatemalan Revolution of 1920

In 1917 an earthquake not only caused a great deal of Guatemala City to collapse into ruins, it also indirectly contributed to the mobilization of anti–Estrada Cabrera forces throughout Guatemala. During the crisis, the United States provided humanitarian aid to the republic, but the corruption-riddled Estrada Cabrera regime prevented much of it from reaching the large numbers of citizens whose most basic needs were being neglected. As a result of the government's failure to provide for anyone but its own clients, conservative opposition forces, including large numbers of Guatemalan IRCA workers, mobilized to overturn the Estrada Cabrera regime.

IRCA workers first entered the body politic that year under the umbrella of the Worker's League. Silverio Ortiz Rivas, a Latin American tailor, founded the artisan-based union and established a reputation for himself as a leading figure in working-class politics in Guatemala City. In June 1919, Ortiz organized a petition drive in the capital to call for the release of leading dissidents. He instructed league members to arrange for the collection of signatures at the central railroad station in the capital; in doing so, he fostered contact between organized workers in the city and railroad workers from the rural provinces.[1]

As early as 1913, IRCA laborers had talked about organizing themselves and workers in other industries. It was not until the period from 1917 to 1920, however, that they took the name the Railroad Workers' League (RWL). IRCA workers in Escuintla on the Pacific coast seem to have organized the first railroad worker's union under this name, between the fall and winter of 1920. Perhaps they took this name in order to identify themselves with the Guatemala City–based Workers' League, because, soon after, the two organizations began working together within the Unionist Party movement to end the Estrada Cabrera dictatorship.

The executive committee of the RWL operated out of Escuintla, with chapters in Puerto Barrios and Zacapa.[2] The organization of the RWL on the Caribbean coast of Guatemala marked an important shift in the history of labor politics within the multiethnic and multinational workforce that had arrived there between the 1880s and the 1920s. As we have seen, foreign migrant workers had dominated earlier, multiethnic episodes of worker militancy, and these episodes had been characterized by their informality and by the absence of a trade union to manage the strikers and set goals. Following the organization of the RWL, however, worker militancy on the Caribbean coast would largely be dominated by Latin Americans, and it would often pit Latin Americans against black workers as well as against United Fruit.

Another group of opponents to Estrada Cabrera began organizing in December 1919: in preparation for the centennial celebration of Central America's independence from the Spanish Crown in 1821, a wealthy group of Guatemalans in the capital had organized the Unionist Party. Benton McMillin, the U.S. minister to Guatemala, reported to Washington that the party was dedicated "to combat[ing] the present reactionary and unprogressive Government," which was affiliated with the Liberal Party.[3] Over time, the Unionist Party became less covert about its agenda, and especially about its opposition to Estrada Cabrera and his flunkies in the Guatemalan National Assembly. It challenged the president's reelection campaign and accused him of engaging in electoral fraud after he was reelected for a new term to run from 1919 until 1923.

After much intense and divisive debate, the Worker's League allied with the Unionist Party, which had quickly established itself as the leading opposition force in Guatemala and whose leaders had money and talent.[4] The Unionist Party reached outside of its Conservative ranks to the Guatemalan working class in order to increase its base of support and protect itself from identification with the old—and greatly disliked—Conservative Party.[5]

The Unionist Party's leadership was conservative; however, its platform supported progressive ideas—free speech, a free press, and civil rights—in a country accustomed to unprogressive government. In addition, Unionists wanted to demilitarize Guatemala by reducing the size of its army of 25,000 troops which spent more time policing than protecting the country.[6] Popular support increasingly played a role in advancing the party's platform. As early as October 1919, the active alliance between the Unionist Party and the Workers' League had begun to spread from the capital to other parts of the republic. Native-born railroad workers on the Caribbean coast already constituted some of the most heavily mobilized laborers in the country. Perhaps this explains why some of the earliest signs of Unionist Party organization appeared in railroad communities. Unionist leaders communicated with departmental workers, who then organized local chapters and kept abreast of party developments. Using flyers to spread the word, rural workers organized about fourteen chapters of the Unionist Party in Zacapa and Izabal.[7]

Working-class support for the Unionists arose in a region that was a political stronghold for Estrada Cabrera. His nephew, Colonel Alberto García, was the longtime governor of Izabal, and Estrada Cabrera's Liberal Party had established an organization, the Liberal Club, in Puerto Barrios in 1915, with the express purpose of mobilizing Izabal voters for Estrada Cabrera and his clients. Members of the Liberal Party had already organized a similar club in nearby Livingston, Izabal, and both clubs planned to work together for the reelection of Estrada Cabrera.[8]

By the winter of 1920 the Liberal Clubs of Izabal were having to compete with radical elements within the Unionist Party movement—mobilized in the newly founded Railroad Worker's League—for control of Caribbean coast politics. Through the members of this league the Unionist movement stoked opposition to Estrada Cabrera's reelection throughout Izabal and into Zacapa. Luis Estrada Monzón, Alberto García's successor as governor of Izabal and a member of the Liberal Party, believed that all IRCA workers belonged to the league, and that it was likely that they sympathized with the Unionist Party as well. Estrada Monzón described the league as being nationalistic yet influenced by and linked to radical labor movements in Mexico. The governor believed that Guatemalan workers were engaged in an evolving "struggle not towards the most lewd form of socialism but toward bolshevism."[9] He tried to repress the opposition forces in Izabal by arresting Unionist Party leaders in that department. Estrada Monzón miscalculated the extent of Unionist support, however; large crowds protested the arrest of the party leaders and demanded the removal of the governor from office, and Monzón was forced into exile in nearby Belize.[10] After Monzón's escape, 250 Unionist men, some of them former IRCA employees, mobilized and marched on the local military barracks, which housed a colonel and twenty-two Guatemalan soldiers; IRCA officials, along with the U.S. vice-consul, facilitated the peaceful abandonment of the barracks on April 10. Unionist supporters also sought to control Puerto Barrios. On April 15, Unionist forces mobilized again, this time to march into the banana plantation region of Quiriguá. They met with no resistance from government forces.[11]

By 1920, Unionist Party leaders could claim twenty-five thousand supporters, but they still had to contend with the threat of U.S. military intervention and a lack of political recognition. More interested in regional stability and the protection of U.S.-owned enterprises than in supporting the spread of democracy and human rights, U.S. State Department officials in Washington and Guatemala supported the repressive Liberal Party of Estrada Cabrera.[12] U.S. representatives in Guatemala, like Ambassador Mc-Millin, claimed to desire a peaceful solution to Guatemala's political conflict and warned that Washington would not recognize any revolutionary government that forcefully removed Estrada Cabrera from power. Most English and American nationals in Guatemala favored the Unionists but avoided overt political affiliation.[13]

Unionist supporters also had to contend with the brutality of Estrada Cabrera's government. From the earliest days of the Unionist Party, government operatives had arrested and tortured party leaders, destroyed opposition printing presses, and murdered an unspecified number of activists.[14] Still, by January 1920, McMillin's informants believed that if the Unionist Party was "not checked within thirty days, at the outside, it will have reached such dimensions, that if the present government attempts to put it down by force, nobody will obey the order."[15]

Popular support for the party was creating a democratic opening in the Guatemalan body politic, as events in Guatemala City and Izabal illustrate. The party's supporters were becoming increasingly numerous, and the government's security apparatus was finding it difficult to repress their activities. For the first time in the long violent history of the Estrada Cabrera dictatorship, McMillin observed, people "on the streets express their opinion openly, with no fear of being overheard." When the National Assembly reconvened in March 1920, rumor had it that "large proportions" of the deputies had distanced themselves from the dictator. Estrada Cabrera had lost an important base of support in the assembly, and his removal from office became virtually inevitable.[16]

In April, in an attempt to diffuse the dangerous political situation, Estrada Cabrera cautioned Guatemalans to maintain public order, proposed salary increases for public-sector employees, and promised free presidential elections in 1922.[17] But it was too late for the dictator to salvage his presidency: in allegiance with dissidents within the National Assembly, Unionist leaders eventually agreed to make Liberal Party member Carlos Herrera y Luna, an army general, wealthy landowner, and a member of the Guatemalan oligarchy, the acting president of Guatemala, an office he held from April to September 1920. He then served as president from September 1920 to December 1921.[18] Unionists conceded four out of six seats in Herrera's cabinet to Liberal appointees, in exchange for the promise of democratic presidential elections in 1922. In addition, they gained freedom for political prisoners, amnesty for those who had been deported, and the free exercise of civil rights as guaranteed by the constitution.[19]

Unionist and Liberal Party representatives spoke English to one another during the several days of negotiations, to keep the less-educated Unionists who represented the Guatemalan working class from influencing the final agreement. As a result, conservatives within the Unionist leadership negotiated the end of the Estrada Cabrera government in exchange for not initiating revolutionary changes in Guatemalan liberalist and militarist policies. For their part, the Liberal Party brought the Estrada Cabrera dictatorship to an end with relatively little armed resistance, except from extremists within the old Conservative Party, a number of whom fought in the capital in support of Estrada Cabrera for eight days following the signing of the accord.[20]

The 1920 Railroad Strike

Under Herrera, the situation of Guatemalan workers improved a little; according to one historian, "People breathed a little more freedom and this logically made it possible for the formation of new organizations."[21] Carlos Herrera's elevation to the presidency sparked a groundswell of labor organizing and unionization as he tried to foster some semblance of workers' rights in Guatemala, promising workers medical services and the right to strike legally, among other things. Herrera's government, in one historian's words, "ignited the courage and energy" of labor organizers, socialists, and communists in Guatemala.[22]

During Herrera's brief presidency, Caribbean coastal workers organized around the fundamental working-class issues that Unionist Party leaders had consistently ignored during their movement against the Estrada Cabrera regime.[23] In May 1920, Guatemalan employees of IRCA in Puerto Barrios went on strike. They demanded that the company increase their salaries substantially, "pay overtime wages, and establish a rigorous promotion scale based on seniority and competence," but IRCA management ignored their demands.[24] Thereafter, the strike spread from Puerto Barrios to other parts of the IRCA railway, and additional Guatemalan railroad men walked off the job. The strikers came to the bargaining table, demanding a living wage, overtime pay, and a say in setting the criteria used for promoting and firing employees.[25] Their control of the railway gave them considerable leverage over their employers and the state: by halting the most important shipping routes, from the provincial food-producing regions on the Caribbean and Pacific coasts to the capital, and from coffee- and banana-producing regions to Puerto Barrios and San José, they were able to do considerable damage to the national economy and to UFCO's bottom line.

In early June 1920, the Guatemala City paper *La Patria* framed the strike in Bolshevik and nationalist terms, calling it a war between the American "capitalists that control the railroads" and the "Guatemalans that serve as the subordinate employees." The paper argued that Guatemalan employees worked "excessively," in exchange for very small salaries, but it also observed, "It is also necessary that the employees moderate their demands a little in courtesy of the general good." The paper acknowledged the class exploitation of Guatemalan workers but challenged them to place national interest above class interest.[26] The 1920 IRCA strike provoked a public debate in Guatemala about the best ways for workers to express their grievances. On this issue, *La Patria* identified three schools of thought: Catholics, who favored "the ascension of the working class by legal and pacifist means"; socialists, who supported workers' ascension by "every means possible"; and extreme leftists, who were anxious to organize an armed revolution.[27] Indeed, it seems possible that the Russian and Mexican revolutions influenced the attitudes of workers in Guatemala, whose leaders, quotted in *La Patria,* increasingly sounded like Bolshevik ideologues.

Both U.S. and Guatemalan officials wanted to curb the influence of leftists, who threatened to infiltrate local labor movements and transform them into a larger, proletarian struggle for the establishment of a socialist state in Guatemala. In early June 1920, Guatemalan officials increased troop presence at the central railroad station in Guatemala City. According to Ambassador McMillin, the government wanted to scare the strikers into returning to work. McMillin added, "The same unrest and striking that impedes progress elsewhere is here with prospect of taking deep root."[28] McMillin seemed to be referring to Bolsheviks, who were commonly blamed for having incited the Mexican and Russian revolutions.

After seven days of complete railroad paralysis, a "happy solution" ended the strike on June 8, 1920. Two high-ranking members of the Unionist Party, Doctor Julio Bianchi and Eduardo Camacho, played an invaluable mediating role, brokering a compromise satisfactory to "all of the railroad personnel, as well as the Company, who, in the way of its possibilities, accepted the just demands of its employees." *La Patria* credited the successful end of the strike to "the enormous influence" of the Unionist Party in Guatemala.[29] The Unionists scrambled to end the strike and thereby reduce the substantial influence that IRCA workers could exercise over the economy. Party leaders did not want to appear weak before the public, nor did they want to share political power with radical members of the RWL.[30]

The labor peace following the Unionist-negotiated summer strike settlement lasted only four months. In the fall of 1920 IRCA officials complained about slowdowns and the low productivity of workers. IRCA's corporate tycoon, Minor Keith, told the Guatemalan minister of development that outside labor agitators had stirred up intransigence among Guatemalan IRCA machinists, making repairs and renovations much more difficult to complete. In addition, he said that following the strike settlement, Guatemalan IRCA employees were earning more but working less. As a solution to the company's labor problems, Keith decided to import foreign workers to repress the organizing efforts of the seasoned railroad workers on the Caribbean coast.[31] Since IRCA's seasoned employees had gone to some lengths to displace foreign workers less than a decade earlier, Keith's attempt understandably led to nativist responses from IRCA's Guatemalan employees, especially those associated with the RWL.[32] In December 1920, Guatemalan newspapers and organizations, including *La Patria* and the *Patriotic League*, continued to openly express disapproval of foreigners. Members of the Puerto Barrios RWL advertised similar sentiments.

Meanwhile, Guatemalan oligarchs began to take the steps necessary to remove President Herrera from power.[33] In December 1921, Unionists installed General José María Orellana Pinto as Estrada Cabrera's successor. Like Estrada Cabrera, Orellana had little tolerance for leftist politics; he had, on one occasion, deported a group of Mexican organizers for spreading Bolshevik teachings. In addition, he threatened to draft any IRCA laborer who refused to obey a return-to-work order into the Guatemalan military. "With all its comparative liberality," journalist Harry Foster wrote, "the new regime was ruling with an iron hand characteristic of Guatemalan governments."[34]

Latin American laborers for IRCA had gained some ground, but true revolutionary progress remained out of reach.

Radicalism and Anti-Americanism on the Caribbean Coast

In an influential 1936 study, historian Charles Kepner argued that no unions existed among banana, railroad, or dockworkers in the 1920s. Kepner described the labor organizations of that time period as impotent, and he said strikes that occurred during the twenties were "sporadic walkouts" that company officials easily undermined "by playing white and black workers against each other."[35] But more recent work has shown that radical movements in the Americas of the 1920s were not a complete failure. During that decade, the radicalism of the Russian Revolution fueled labor politics throughout the Western world, including the Americas. In Panama, workers mobilized and used the strike to establish collective bargaining rights. Similar developments occurred among North American workers: in 1919, four million laborers from various trades staged some three thousand strikes across the United States.[36] West Indian World War I veterans returned to Central America radicalized from their experiences fighting for democracy and self-determination in the British Army. In Costa Rica, the West Indian press on the Caribbean coast provided a venue for workers' interests and a forum for the spread of labor organizing. Indeed, returning veterans and the press spread subversive ideas to various parts of the Caribbean region. Travelers brought information and firsthand accounts of events from all over the globe.[37]

After the disappointment of the 1920 revolution, Guatemalan workers abandoned their alliances with the capitalist class and turned inward. Laborers, like the IRCA railroaders, strengthened their own working-class institutions and waged class-based struggles for the good of laborers and their families. Members of the Guatemalan RWL developed alliances with the Mexican RWL and the Federation of Panamerican Workers and increased the influence of their union throughout various IRCA departments in Guatemala.

As in Mexico, Guatemalan workers first developed a functional labor organization during the outbreak of a revolutionary movement to overthrow a U.S.-supported dictator. After the revolution failed to address their demands, laborers resorted to strikes against the U.S.-owned IRCA. Now a more militant workforce, the RWL demanded a living wage and greater input in company decisions. Following the lead of the Mexican railroad brotherhoods, the RWL in Guatemala also championed the end of foreign domination of better-paying railroad jobs and the expulsion of foreign workers, especially North Americans. In an attempt to repress the increasingly radical IRCA workforce, whose right to organize UFCO and IRCA refused to acknowledge, Minor C. Keith tried to bring in replacement workers from outside Guatemala. The decision to use replacement workers unleashed a nationalist backlash from RWL members against company officials. RWL strikes signaled to Caribbean coast workers in other industries that collective action could be used to influence the decisions that affected their daily lives.[38]

In the period following the 1920 revolution, unions proliferated among Guatemalan workers. Caribbean coast IRCA employees joined forces with railroad workers in the Pacific coast town of Escuintla to establish the Unión Ferrocarrilera de Guatemala (the Guatemalan Railroad Workers' Union, or RWU). Its relationship to the RWL is unclear. Those who did not work for the railroad organized and supported other unions, such as the Laborers and Workers of Puerto Barrios and the Caribbean Dockworkers' League. All three unions were founded in 1921.[39] Following the lead of workers in Honduras, other parts of Latin America, and Europe, moreover, some Guatemalan laborers in the capital founded the Union Obrera Socialista in 1921, and the Communist Party of Central America, Guatemalan Section, around 1922.[40]

In 1920, as we have seen, the revolutionary overthrow of dictator Estrada Cabrera in Guatemala marked a surge in unionism and radicalism, especially in the capital city. The Federation of Guatemalan Workers (Federación Obrera de Guatemala), a national union that apparently included members of the RWL, had the largest membership among the new labor organizations. But starting with the presidency of Carlos Herrera in 1921 it became committed to working within the system and received government subsidies.[41] Labor organization in Guatemala City, in the words of one historian, "neither had the manpower nor the resources" to make more than slight inroads into the Caribbean coast workforce. This left Caribbean coast labor movements to develop independently from the objectives and tactics of labor organizations in the capital.[42] While capital city labor movements did fuel labor organization and radical thought, they had the disadvantage of being located in the interior under the close watch of right-wing governments. Because the banana industry relied on a transportation infrastructure that was both interior (railroad lines) and external (port shipping), Caribbean coast workers in general tended to be more exposed to radicalism than their urban counterparts in interior regions of Central America. Outsiders who traveled from one Caribbean port to another therefore exerted the greatest influence on lowland workers, far from the watchful eyes of government conservatives.

Historian Charles Berquist argues that export-oriented worker movements were more successful because local laborers who challenged foreign capital had the ability to mobilize "the powerful sentiment of patriotism" among propagandists and the elite.[43] After the resignation of the Mexican dictator Porfirio Díaz in May 1911, for example, there were times during the Mexican Revolution when anti-imperialist reactions to U.S.-owned railroad companies "cut across class lines" and permitted brief alliances between the government and Mexican workers.[44] One scholar of the region found that in the early twentieth century the cultural nationalism of Latin American revolutionaries from Mexico to Brazil "looked toward previously despised races for the source of their countries' identity." UFCO's black workforce, however, became an impediment to anti-imperialist accusations of labor exploitation. Over time, therefore, Hispanic Costa Rican workers started to link foreign black workers with white company officials as the source of their hardships.[45] Similarly, Guatemalan workers on the Caribbean coast in the 1920s saw themselves as patriotic citizens willing to challenge North American imperialism (although few Guatemalan oligarchs were willing to join in that struggle). Like Costa Rican nationals, Guatemalan workers identified English-speaking British and North American workers with the company.[46]

At the start of 1921, the Railroad Workers' League on the Caribbean coast joined in solidarity with the Railroad Workers' League of Mexico, with the hope of gaining, in the words of the governor of Izabal, "the expulsion of the North American employees."[47] Soon thereafter, Izabal officials questioned some IRCA workers about the RWL meetings and agendas. The workers told the police that "the league between Guatemala and Mexico is very strong" and that workers in both countries were mobilizing to expel "all the North American company employees."[48] Samuel Gompers, U.S. labor leader and president of the Federation of Panamerican Workers (FPW), apparently heard of the nationalistic labor movements gaining momentum in the region. He arrived in Mexico City just after New Year's Day in 1921 with the "principal proposal" of developing "good relations between the workers of the United States of America, Mexico, and Central America." Gompers organized an FPW meeting in Mexico City in which delegates from sixteen republics in Central and South America, including FPW workers from the United States and Mexico, discussed their concerns and differences.[49] After several hours of debate, Gompers was narrowly reelected president of the FPW. FPW leaders selected Guatemala City as the site for the organization's next annual meeting.[50]

If Gompers's goal was to keep Latin American workers from turning against North Americans, however, his mission failed: following the 1921 FPW meeting in Mexico City, RWL members developed an increasingly global working-class consciousness, but this perception was steeped in an anti-imperialist ideology that championed the end of U.S. domination in the Caribbean and Central America. At the local level in Izabal and Zacapa, RWL members called for an end to the foreign monopoly on better-paying jobs.[51] The committee increasingly came to IRCA officials with complaints revolving around difficulties that "constantly" occurred between North American supervisors and Guatemalan subordinates. Trouble arose when IRCA general manager Alfred Clark replaced manager Jaime Peralta with the less competent and more arrogant Juan J. Machado. Clark made this important personnel change without consulting the RWL, and he failed to explain the rationale for his unpopular decision. IRCA's unionized workers petitioned for Peralta's return. Clark ignored the request. In early February 1921, the governor of Izabal described the men as "very restless and eager to take revenge."[52]

The 1921 Railroad Strike

Soon after the unsuccessful petition, rumors spread that the RWL would organize a strike to demand the expulsion of U.S. supervisors and work-ers. Workers organized a meeting in the Pacific coast town of Escuintla. Informants reported that fired manager Peralta was arranging "organizing sessions" in his Escuintla home and that former IRCA employee Enrique Barillas and others had initiated the nationalist movement.[53] In late April 1921, members of the Escuintla Railroad Workers Union sent telegrams to Puerto Barrios declaring their solidarity with the Caribbean division and demanding Machado's dismissal.[54] Around the same time, RWU division executive committee member Víctor M. Corantes sent a telegram to Clark threatening a general strike on the Northern Railroad branch of IRCA. The RWU demanded Machado's removal, arguing that based on "competence and seniority there are honorable employees" more deserving of the posi-tion.[55] The workers were tired of the company's inflexible position that dic-tated that employees had no right to collective bargaining or participation in the company's decision-making process.[56] In his response to Corantes, Clark stated that the company would not "guarantee the dismissal of Machado, nor guarantee that those that have taken active part in the strike . . . will not be punished." As a result of Clark's hard line, the RWU executive committee declared a general work stoppage."[57]

The militancy of the workers inspired Clark to do some research on the RWU leaders. IRCA officials organized a detailed list containing the names, positions, and occupations of the Guatemalan division of the RWU executive committee. The research showed that Guatemalan railroad men from diverse occupations filled leadership positions within the RWU: artisans, service-sector workers, an engineer, two conductors, and a storekeeper. An IRCA informant reported that the RWU had branches in both the town of Zacapa and in Puerto Barrios.[58]

As the strike progressed, city residents increasingly complained about food shortages and other hardships caused by the strike. In its April 26, 1921, edition, *El Diario* reported that in the capital the "survivors" of the strike raised the prices of scarce goods, such as milk, coming from the rural departments. In general, the paper reported, the capital's working class had suffered and protested most about the reduced availability of food. These same inconveniences often did not affect the strikers and their families, because they lived in areas that provided much of the capital's meat and dairy supply.[59] Eventually, the economic fallout of the strike persuaded the minister of development to call both sides to the bargaining table.[60] The workers reiterated their position that they would not return to work without the removal of Machado and the return of Peralta. Against the wall, Clark accepted the principal demands of the strikers, on the condition that in the future union representatives would name a delegate who would first discuss disagreements directly with the company. If that failed, the issue would be brought before the minister of development. Additional details of the settlement included the continued employment of all strikers at the end of the dispute.[61]

The 1923 Dock Strike

During the early 1920s Guatemalan newspapers carried on a lively debate about the direction of labor unions globally and nationally. The decidedly pro-labor newspaper *Excelsior* published a March 1922 article that argued that unions and working-class solidarity represented the "key" to the "intellectual" development and "prosperity" of Guatemalan society.[62] Similarly, another March 1922 article, by a mechanic named Reniero, cautioned Guatemalan workers against incorporating "counter-productive" theories from other countries. Instead, Reniero challenged workers to study and apply well-thought-out strategies applicable to conditions in Guatemala: "Our Unionism needs schools, instruction, books, magazines, lecture rooms, libraries, conferences; above all Political Economy or the science of wealth whose primary instrument of production is work."[63] A May 1922 article in *Excelsior* provides evidence that workers in Guatemala had a comprehensive worldview born of the period's radicalism. The article stated, "In the United States there are four million worker stoppages, in Great Britain close to three million and in the rest of the industrial nations" workers are striking for the end of wage reduction and demanding higher wages.[64] *Excelsior* followed this with a September 1922 article that championed the right and obligation of workers to participate in national and foreign politics. The article argued that workers should not serve as instruments of the wealthy, who seek power for their personal benefit. Working-class politics should focus on "defending the interest of the Motherland" and defending the interest of unions. The article added: "For the defense of both, the workers have to separate themselves from the capitalist aristocracy, and construct the organization of workers under the most advanced and liberal principals, conscious of the important factors of social evolution and not machines for the bidding of the President and enriching the caudillos."[65]

It is within this political context that workers on the Caribbean coast organized the region's most comprehensive labor strike. On February 3, 1923, dockworkers Julio Molina, Genaro Ochoa, and a majority of workers at Puerto Barrios announced to the Guatemalan minister of development Rafael Ponciane: "Today at six in the morning we declared a passive strike, in virtue of the fact that for many years we have been giving our work to the United Fruit Company while harming our women and children."[66] As the 1923 strike developed, organizers from Honduras and El Salvador appeared to help organize UFCO workers. Company informants reported that Salvadorans who lived in Puerto Barrios's "red light district" served as the "principal strike leaders." The strike began with some two hundred men in support. Two days later, the strikers' ranks swelled to a diverse group of four hundred from all occupations. Dockworkers, shop personnel, and carpenters all united by their near servitude to United Fruit. One of the first protests involved blocking the passage of a train to the dock. The four hundred workers reportedly preferred "to die" than give up on their cause.[67]

By February 10, U.S. chargé d'affaires Arthur Geissler wrote the U.S. secretary of state that eight hundred Guatemalan farm laborers at Quiriguá had also joined the strike. They demanded higher wages and the end of preferences for two thousand African American plantation workers, most of whom came from Belize and Jamaica.[68] The company's predominately

African American contingent of banana plantation workers still had not joined their Guatemalan coworkers in supporting the strike. Neither had the predominately Guatemalan nationals working for IRCA. As the strike spread across UFCO's entire Guatemalan division, workers seized company facilities, including an electric plant at Quiriguá. They also prevented three hundred African American workers, whom company officials had brought from UFCO plantations, from moving freight between United Fruit Company railroad cars and the ships docked at Puerto Barrios.[69]

UFCO officials later reassigned three hundred banana plantation workers to the docks at Puerto Barrios. They ordered the replacement workers to load a UFCO steamship with recently harvested banana stems. According to Jorge Ferguson, a suspected labor agitator from Puerto Barrios, UFCO arranged to use replacement workers to end the strikes that were developing throughout the different divisions. The company's strategy was to force the majority of the workers to eventually cross the picket line.[70] Strike leaders Molina and Ochoa showed up to talk workers out of crossing the picket line. As the two men tried to win over the replacement workers, the port superintendent called a Puerto Barrios policeman and had them arrested. In addition, governor Santiago Quiñónez "dispatched armed government troops and policemen" to Puerto Barrios.[71]

Quiñónez, said UFCO manager Thomas, "had a short talk" with both Molina and Ochoa and then released them from custody. "A few minutes later they were back on the wharf using every means in their power, including force, to tie up the pier," Thomas reported, adding, "It of course only took them a short while to make the tie-up complete and get every-one to leave the pier and ship." Later that same day, two hundred striking workers "threw switches in front of the train, uncoupled all the cars, [and] stoned and attacked the men on board them to prevent the unloading and loading of banana stems." Thomas continued: "All this occurred in broad daylight within a few hundred feet of the railway station, and right in front of armed government troops, and policemen, who took no steps to handle the situation." Under cover of night, Thomas managed to get almost all the company's farmhands to the dock. However, the strikers continued to resist attempts to load pierside vessels. The workers demonstrated a similar resolve in stopping the movement of the railroad fruit cars used to transport the stems from the banana plantations to the dock at Puerto Barrios.[72] IRCA officials found that several hundred strikers had practically commandeered seventy cars of fruit in the railway yards at Puerto Barrios, thereby preventing their movement. The strikers used force to stop several IRCA attempts to switch the fruit cars in question.

In addition, according to UFCO's Thomas, fifty armed strikers "took charge of our engine 43 at Quiriguá, and forced the engineer, an American, to take them all around the plantation railway lines." He added, "They stopped at laborers' camps and instructed all laborers to stop work at once, stating further that those who refused to would be killed."[73] The workers then directed the train to the company's divisional headquarters at Bananera and, likewise, threatened any worker who dared to continue laboring during the strike. Similar incidents occurred when two hundred armed strikers converged on other areas of the "Bananera Line."[74] The fact that the strikers committed "lawless acts of violence" with total impunity in front of armed soldiers, army officers, "and on many occasions" the *comandante* of the Puerto Barrios garrison himself infuriated Thomas. More than once, company officials had requested that governor Quiñónez "clear the railway yard of strikers, and mobs of strikers, but he persistently refused to do so, saying that the Railway yard was public property, and that strikers had a perfect right to use the same."[75] Quiñónez's behavior suggests his sympathy for the striking workers. Some of those local and national Guatemalan officials who came into office during the 1920 revolution owed their positions to workers in Zacapa and Puerto Barrios, who had organized chapters of the Unionist Party and supported the revolution on the Caribbean coast. For this reason, some Unionist Party members in public office in Guatemala City and on the Caribbean coast supported the workers during labor disputes. The seeming collaboration of the governor with the strikers aided the workers in their challenge to UFCO's usually unfettered dominance over the banana enclave and company employees. By the third day of the strike, a small group of militant labor organizers had mobilized the UFCO workforce and had virtually shut down the entire UFCO Guatemalan division.[76]

Strike leader Molina sent a petition to Guatemalan president Orellana asking him to designate a judge who would serve as the government mediator to settle the Caribbean coast labor dispute and, in the words of one of the strike leaders, would "represent a favorable solution which we hope for." In the petition, the workers escalated their demands beyond their earlier call for increased wages. They demanded an equal division of work between Guatemalans and Jamaicans, a salary increase (one cent instead of a half a cent for stevedores loading bananas), overtime wages for "extraordinary days," and the calculation of ordinary work time "from the moment the worker receives the Ticket [and begins to start his assigned lot of bananas to load]."[77] Workers demanded a simplification of the "forms that facilitate the entrance to Quiriguá Hospital" for all patients, the hiring of Guatemalan physicians at the Quiriguá Hospital, and free medical care and medicine for dockworkers at Puerto Barrios. They also demanded company-furnished dormitories for single dockworkers and huts for those with families. The housing demand was a benefit that the company already provided to its employees on all banana plantations. In short, dockworkers wanted to be treated the same as plantation employees.[78]

As the strike continued, worker demands expanded to include demands for a radical change in the relationship between UFCO and the people of Guatemala.[79] For example, during the second week of the strike, Salvadoran strike leader Genaro Ochoa wrote Guatemalan minister of development Rafael Ponciane on behalf of the striking workers. He demanded that the government force UFCO to start paying taxes reflecting the profits it earned from its Guatemalan enterprises. It disturbed workers that former president Estrada Cabrera had in 1901 granted UFCO a number of concessions that were "disastrous" for Guatemalans. Ochoa's letter also protested the monopoly enjoyed by UFCO's "Great White Fleet" over the use of Puerto Barrios and the import and export of goods between the United States and Guatemala. "The railroad Company owns the Puerto Barrios dock and has the exclusive right" to dock construction on all points along the Caribbean coast, said the letter. The workers argued that allowing a private entity to control the docks went against the citizens' economic and political interests. They viewed the concessions granted to UFCO as unconstitutional and harmful to the commercial freedom of both the United States and Guatemala. They added, "We want a general benefit for the habitants of both countries, that ends these abnormal conditions that oppose such a noble end."[80]

Strike leaders also denounced the company for not paying the government any monthly or yearly taxes or rent for its vast holdings on the Caribbean coast. Finally, the workers complained that the company evicted Guatemalan squatters from lands that the government reserved for public use. UFCO then used this illegally wrested land to develop plantations in Izabal. Strike demands centered on an anti-imperialist and class analyses. In the words of striking laborer Andrés H. Morales: "When they exploit us and treat us like work animals, it is clear that we seek the method of improving our situation by the method universally recognized as the protector of the working class, this is an appeal to the strike [as a] . . . radical solution to impart justice and establish equilibrium between capital and the worker."[81]

On February 14, 1923, federal officials in Guatemala City sent General Enrique Aris to investigate the conduct of Governor Quiñónez and his subordinates during the strike.[82] Caribbean coast residents knew Aris, the former governor of the department of Zacapa, for his "cruel and blood thirsty" treatment of foreigners and Guatemalan nationals. His reputation as an en-

emy of the working class made him perfectly suited to repress the labor conflict in Izabal. According to the workers, General Aris criticized governor
Quiñónez and worked under the direction of UFCO officials, who hosted
him in the company's hotel with company employees attending to his every
need. Quiñónez, workers insisted, had remained fair and loyal to the government and had refused company bribes. Writing to the Ministry of War and
the Ministry of Government and Justice some two weeks into the strike, the
workers asked that Quiñónez be allowed to keep his position.[83] Meanwhile,
UFCO spared no expense in lobbying General Aris to side with the company
in his investigation of the labor dispute. Against the workers' wishes, Aris
quickly replaced Quiñónez as the governor of the department. Of Aris's new
leadership, the workers said, "his tyrannical proceedings" firmly marked him
as an offensive and "fearful terrorist of emphatic manner," who had "come
threatening to imprison the pacifistic habitants."[84] The general's actions created hatred and distrust of the government among the laborers and the residents of Izabal. The workers said quite simply that it was because Aris was
"naturally a tyrant."[85]

Strike leaders began holding meetings and appointing delegates to address such concerns as the abuses suffered under General Aris. By mid-February 1923, *El Imparcial* reported that delegates from the Puerto Barrios
workers had traveled to Guatemala City to meet with President Orellana and
representatives from the two labor organizations. After a meeting between
the UFCO laborers and the Guatemalan president, labor leaders decided to
accept mediation by a government-appointed body. "The principal demand,"
according to U.S. chargé d'affaires Arthur Geissler, "appears to be for an
increase in the compensation for loading bananas." UFCO paid workers at
Puerto Barrios a half-cent per bunch. The strikers were asking for one cent.
UFCO paid one cent for similar work in Honduras, and paid as much as one-
and-a-half cents in Costa Rica.[86]

Under pressure to get laborers back to work, labor representatives from
Izabal accepted the mediation of the government body. In addition, they
ordered their coworkers to return to work as the talks continued, as a sign of
their "willingness to negotiate in good faith." In response, Orellana promised
the workers the "protection" and "collaboration" of the "Supreme Government" during the talks. Meanwhile, UFCO's Thomas demanded the evic-
tion of all strikers who remained on company land or buildings in order to
make room for replacement workers.[87] In the words of the laborers, General
Aris tried "to impose [his] despotic will on the workers" and favored the
company's interests. Aris also ordered paramilitaries to "commit many il-

legal and arbitrary acts on the docks, plantations, and even in the town of Quiriguá."[88]

In late February 1923, *El Imparcial* reported that workers had organized a ten-person board of directors. The ten leaders all had Latin American surnames. The board's first act was to address the dictatorial conduct of General Aris before the Metropolitan Commission (composed of representatives from the government and labor unions from Guatemala City). As talks continued into the month of March between union, state, and company representatives, UFCO officials—still refusing to recognize the workers' right to collective bargaining—hired replacement workers.[89] *El Imparcial* reported on rumors from the negotiating sessions that the company would not capitulate to union demands and was refusing to agree to a raise of even a quarter of a percent.[90] Meanwhile, the workers gave up their demand that the company end its favored hiring and treatment of English-speaking workers.[91]

To pressure the company to move beyond its intransigence, President Orellana apparently arranged a meeting between his minister of development, Rafael Ponciane, and UFCO superintendent Rufus K. Thomas.[92] In a UFCO company memorandum, Thomas reported that during the almost ninety-minute meeting, Ponciane was polite yet "openly antagonistic to the Company, to foreigners in general, and more than sympathetic with labor unions, and their demands, and the position which he took on many matters was nothing short of Bolshevism." The Guatemalan official pressured Thomas to formally recognize the workers' right to organize and bargain collectively. In the unfolding struggles throughout the world between capital and labor of the 1920s, Ponciane argued, unless concessions could be made to worker demands, "the Government would be powerless" to stop four to five thousand disgruntled workers. Ponciane, according to Thomas, also argued that "a government must always be on the side of its own citizens," and that multinational corporations should not expect the country's military to act on behalf of foreign capital against national workers.[93]

By March 1923 it was clear to U.S. chargé d'affaires Arthur Geissler that the Guatemalan government was pressuring UFCO officials to use all of their vast resources to end the strike peacefully.[94] In a report to the U.S. secretary of state, Geissler wrote that President Orellana worried that the strike would spread to other parts of Guatemala and Central America. "Unless the Company negotiates with the men, there will be a general walk-out, extending even into Honduras," Geissler told the U.S. secretary of state. Geissler reported that Orellana "fear[ed] that violence would be unavoidable," and believed that the "demands of the strikers [were] worthy of serious consideration." Orellana remained resolved to "preserve law and order, 'although oppressed by the thought that many poor fellows may have to die.'"[95]

Pressure on Orellana to end the strike intensified in early March, when it became clear that the strikers were ready to unite with opposition leader Marcial Prem. Prem's representation of Guatemala at the U.S.-organized conference of Central American states in December 1922 had bolstered his nationalist reputation. At the conference, he had supported a general peace treaty and friendship between neighboring Central American states, but Prem saw U.S. participation in an investigative commission on international conflict as an unacceptable example of U.S. intervention.[96] Because of Prem's anti-American stance, U.S. officials labeled him a Bolshevik. Secretly, Prem had plotted a military coup against General Orellana's government. Prem was joined by several working-class Guatemalans and a few respected politicians and lawyers in his negative opinion of Orellana's pro–North American stance. The group also accused Orellana of eroding the country's political autonomy.

Rumors abounded that opposition leaders and their supporters planned an armed rebellion, to begin on March 14, 1923. In addition, the president received intelligence reports that on March 14 Caribbean coast workers would wage a sympathy strike in favor of the armed rebellion and as a show of contempt for the government. Orellana sought a peaceful settlement of the Caribbean labor dispute, but by March he had come to see the use of troops as a necessary strategy to address a larger political and armed opposition movement. As the talks between UFCO officials and the workers made little to no progress, General Orellana used the negotiation period to increase the government's military presence in Izabal. On March 5, two railroad cars loaded with soldiers under the command of a Colonel Gabino Cuyun "headed to Puerto Barrios, with the objective of safeguarding the interest of the Company and protecting order." Guatemalan officials appointed General Carlos Jurado as commander of all military operations in the Caribbean region.[97]

In addition, Geissler and Orellana met on March 13 and took steps to prepare for the rumored coup. Orellana published an article in *Excelsior* revealing the government's knowledge of Prem's call for a revolution, Orellana's dismissal of Prem's nationalistic position in support of a revolution, and the general's announcement of the arrival of the USS *Tacoma* at Puerto Barrios on the day of the anticipated revolution. Orellana also dispatched a large number of troops to the Caribbean coast in fear of a Bolshevik-supported revolution.[98] In the final analysis, the strategy worked. Prem and his followers cancelled their call for armed rebellion. On the Caribbean coast, March 14 passed without incident, except for the arrival of the USS *Tacoma*. Geissler invited the commander of the *Tacoma* to visit the U.S. embassy in Guatemala City. Forty-five armed, blue-coated, U.S. sailors accompanied the commander on the IRCA train trip to the capital. In Izabal, officials arrested suspected labor organizers and deported them to Bluefields, Nicaragua. By the end of March, officials had purged the Caribbean coast of some twenty foreign labor leaders, and the dock at Puerto Barrios reopened and operated as they had before the start of the 1923 strike.[99]

The means by which the government finally managed to repress the strike remains sketchy at best. It is evident, however, that the military intervention of both the Guatemalan and U.S. forces proved decisive. As one historian argues, "It was neither the first nor the last time that the government dispatched troops to restore order, but military intervention on this scale had not been seen before."[100] On March 23, 1923, the Guatemalan minister of war reassigned General Aris to an undisclosed post. Banana laborers did not mount another anti-imperialist, anti-monopolist challenge to UFCO until the revolution of 1944.

Labor militancy on the Caribbean coast of Guatemala in the early 1920s further divided the coastal labor force along lines of class, race, and nationality, at the same time that it linked Latin Americans in Guatemala to militant labor movements throughout the region, and particularly to those in Mexico, Honduras, and El Salvador. The events of the 1920 revolution involved an eruption of chaotic and politically charged nationalism in Guatemala.[101] The democratic opening in 1920 inspired Latin American workers to organize, as Carlos Herrera's administration granted laborers rights for the first time since that country's independence from Spain. Yet Herrera's activism on behalf of workers threatened the interests of the national oligarchy that owned the country's coffee and sugar plantations, and as a result, the oligarchs withdraw their support from Herrera and threw it instead behind General José María Orellana Pinto, who remained in office from 1921 to 1926. Orellana and his successor, Lázaro Chacón González, who served as president of Guatemala from 1926 to 1931, both paid lip-service to workers' rights while restricting them in practice.[102] On the Caribbean coast of Guatemala, radicals of various ideologies and complexions used the political opening of the period 1920–21 to build a labor movement that collectively battled for more than just the interests of the working class and that expanded its reach in the period from 1922 to 1923. Guatemalan laborers focused their efforts on higher wages, on expanding opportunities for Latin American workers at the expense of English-speaking workers from North America and the West Indies, and on breaking U.S. control over the country's railroad and the country's president by the use of the strike. That they achieved very few of these goals in the short run does not detract from the importance of their actions for future workers. Yet we should also keep in mind that Latin American laborers' mobilization was predicated to a certain extent on the exclusion of black workers, who would organize a separate struggle for improved working conditions under the banner of Garveyism. It is to the story of that struggle that the next chapter turns.

6

We Depend on Others Too Much

Garveyism and Labor Radicalism in the Caribbean Basin

The benefits of labor incorporation won by Latin American IRCA workers following the 1920 Unionist revolution in Guatemala were predicated to a certain extent on labor's exclusion of black immigrant workers. These workers also mobilized in the early 1920s, but their radicalism was inspired less by regional revolutionary nationalism than by Marcus Garvey's Black Nationalism. Like the Latin American labor radicalism of this period, Garveyism emphasized the global connections among workers, and it encouraged them to band together in a common struggle to succeed. Unlike the radicalism of Latin American railroad and dockworkers in Guatemala, however, Garvey's message was not especially anti-imperialist—indeed, it was pro-capitalist. While Garvey acknowledged the exploitation of black workers around the globe and mobilized these workers on the basis of this acknowledgment, he encouraged working-class black men not to overthrow their employers but to become tycoons themselves. In the Guatemalan context, workers adapted Garvey's message to their needs, using Garveyism as a tool with which to organize and express solidarity—but they also used it to express their grievances and to strike.

Garveyism in the Caribbean

Two weekly newspapers, *The Workman* and the *Negro World*, helped shape the consciousness of black immigrants in the Caribbean basin. Published by the West Indian Protective League, an immigrant association, *The Workman* was a "very pro-British" weekly paper. The black nationalist editors of Marcus Garvey's *Negro World* covered Pan-African problems. Both organs catered to black immigrant communities, on the Caribbean coast of Central America and in different regions of Cuba and elsewhere. The *Negro World's* coverage of events throughout the Pan-African world provided news and inspiration for radical working-class struggles. Published from the fall of 1918 until 1933, the *Negro World* became the most widely read black newspaper in the world, with sections printed in English, Spanish, and French.[1]

Jamaican-born Marcus Garvey had traveled to the Caribbean coast of Costa Rica in 1910 at the age of twenty-one. During his stay, he lived with his maternal uncle, who worked for UFCO. Garvey's uncle found a job for him as a timekeeper on a banana plantation; later, Garvey worked as a dockworker in Puerto Limon, Costa Rica.[2] There, Garvey started a newspaper called *La Nación* to carry his black nationalist views to Costa Ricans. Because of the newspaper, Costa Rican and British authorities labeled Garvey an instigator; neither did UFCO officials view Garvey's activism favorably. Garvey next traveled to Guatemala, Nicaragua, and Panama. During his time in Latin America, Garvey developed an awareness of the region's African diasporas, which included both native-born black people and immigrants from the West Indies and the United States. He eventually returned to Jamaica and founded several black nationalist organizations, before establishing the United Negro Improvement Association (UNIA). As his vision for the UNIA developed, he always included members of Latin America's black diaspora in the organization.[3]

In 1916 Garvey moved the headquarters of the UNIA from Jamaica to Harlem in New York City. The migration of large numbers of blacks from the southern United States and the Caribbean basin during World War I contributed to the growth of the UNIA in North America. Garvey used the *Negro World* to attract followers from around the world to the message of the UNIA.[4] A 1921 speech Garvey gave in Panama and published in the *Negro World* highlights his appeal to immigrants in Central America and his understanding of their circumstances. Garvey said: "The U.N.I.A. is not insular, is not Trinidadian, is not American, is not Parochial, is not Barbadian, is not Jamaican. It is purely a Negro Institution. . . . We recognize anyone as a Negro who has one-sixteenth drop of Negro blood in his veins." Garvey's vision for the UNIA involved building a Pan-African movement for blacks, a government for blacks of all nationalities. In Garvey's words, "The Barbadian can work for it, the Jamaican can work for it, the Americans can work for it, just as you worked for the Panama Canal. Now, there is a similar work for you in Africa." In regard to class differences, Garvey emphasized that there was room for people of all classes in his movement: "Those of you who can lay railroads, who can build buildings, those of you who are educated to be clerks and school teachers will find that work to do and those who are lawyers will practice their law."[5] The glue that united the diverse members of his international movement was racial solidarity. Garvey believed that black people everywhere shared a common struggle against racism. "You cannot

Figure 6.1. United Fruit workers in Panama loading fruit on a steamship

Figure 6.2. United Fruit workers in Puerto Castilla, Honduras, loading fruit, 1920s

get away from race," he explained, continuing: "I do not care how far you go—how far your travels be—you cannot get away from your race. You will have to come back some day or the other. It is only a question of time and we will be driven back to our race."[6]

Garvey articulated a clear understanding of how UFCO officials mistreated blacks in Costa Rica, Guatemala, Nicaragua, and Honduras: they would first employ them to clear land, dam swamps and lagoons, make places sanitary, and tend to and harvest bananas, coffee, and cocoa, and then, he said, they "cut your pay, made your economic conditions harder, and ultimately drove you off the land." According to Garvey, such unsavory practices forced many laborers to move from one republic to another in search of work. Garvey argued that only when black people developed economic and political strength—only when they became share-owning capitalists rather than proletarians—could they end the cycle of worker exploitation. "We have come to the conclusion," said Garvey in the same speech, "that we must concentrate our forces and our energy the same way as we did in the construction of the Panama Canal, and on the plantations in Costa Rica and Guatemala[,] so as to build for ourselves a permanent government of our own in Africa, and thereby not let any government or race decide how much each of us should work for, but show and let them know that we are masters of our own destiny and we will decide our own economical affairs. . . . That," he concluded, "is what the U.N.I.A. seeks to do."[7]

Former UNIA member and employee Hugh Mulzac recalled, "The events which drew me to the Garvey movement in 1920 were also attracting millions of other colored men and women. Chief among them was the outrageous discrimination to which they had been subjected during the [First World War], both in the Army and in civilian jobs." He added, "Race patriotism, the promise of an African renaissance under [black] control, and the attraction of rapidly multiplying dollars drew colored folk to the Garvey movement as they had not been drawn by any other since the Civil War and Reconstruction."[8]

The growth of Garveyism coincided with increasing migration throughout Latin America by West Indian and U.S. blacks.[9] For example, some 22,000 Jamaicans migrated to Cuba between 1911 and 1921, many of them attracted by jobs on sugar plantations. Large numbers of Haitians also traveled there during the same period, many of them on UFCO's "Great White Fleet," a line of steamships that carried bananas, sugar, cacao, and passengers between the principal ports of the United States, the West Indies, and Latin America. In addition to steamship passage, black workers could and did travel by rail and other means of transportation; indeed, improved access to transportation contributed to the mobility of black immigrants throughout the Caribbean basin.[10] Wherever they went, these migrants took the UNIA with them. West Indian, American, and Canadian immigrants in Cuba established fifty-two UNIA branches near black immigrant communities in Santiago de Cuba, Guantánamo, Camaguey, Cepedes, and Oriente de Cuba.[11] Only the state of Louisiana had more branches of the UNIA in one geographic region than did Cuba. The UNIA in Cuba and elsewhere served as the migrant's government, civic association, social club, political action committee, and place of worship.[12]

"The greater Caribbean area (including Central and northern South America)," according to one Garvey scholar, "was undoubtedly the biggest Garveyite stronghold outside of the United States."[13] West Indian immigrants established forty-six branches of the UNIA in the Panama Canal Zone, third in number after the United States and Cuba. Garvey followers also established strongholds wherever West Indian immigrants settled in Panama, Honduras, Colombia, Mexico, Brazil, Ecuador, Venezuela, Guatemala, and Nicaragua.[14]

The UNIA helped unite the diverse black population of Central America. Because it emphasized the mutual reality of race and of second-class treatment, it significantly reduced resentment and competition between people of African descent in Central America. Black immigrant spaces like the UNIA's Liberty Hall served as meeting places where workers organized against their exploiters. UNIA halls provided working-class black immigrants with important gathering places for organizing and advancing a black nationalist agenda that centered on improving conditions for black workers. Notably, they tended to be located in port towns along the Caribbean coastline. Historically, port cities have given working-class residents access to revolutionary ideas and movements from around the world, with which they have developed a local and global radical consciousness. UFCO's "Great White Fleet" regularly docked at Caribbean ports, and the laborers who traveled on its ships carried news about radical workers in other parts of the Atlantic World. In short, black UFCO and IRCA workers were well situated to develop and exchange ideas because residents of port cities had the militant consciousness to support and carry out organized struggles for workers' rights.[15]

The UNIA as an organization was sympathetic to the struggles of laborers, but its central purpose was not to empower black workers or to battle the elite capitalists who employed them. Far from it: Garvey instructed his followers to view white employers as their best friends until they achieved economic freedom. As one historian explains, "Garvey's immediate interest in the Caribbean and in Central America, as well as everywhere else, was building up the Black Star Shipping Line."[16] He founded the Negro Factories Corporation (NFC) and the Black Star Line (BSL) as a means to help black people to achieve economic independence. In a 1921 speech in Cuba, Garvey explained that he envisioned the NFC and BSL as providing the "industrial and commercial strength" necessary for the "elevation of the black race."[17] The NFC provided information and capital for starting and networking black businesses, such as modern steam laundries, haberdasheries, grocery stores, and larger enterprises. The BSL organized the shipment of goods and supplies for members of the NFC.[18] It also provided a needed alternative for black travelers, who suffered myriad insults on white-owned, Jim Crow–operated ships. Personal experience with such indignities helps to explain why so many itinerant black workers in the Caribbean basin became supporters of and shareholders in the BSL. In January 1920, to give one example, a radical Panamanian labor organizer named Morales led a group of blacks in protest of the efforts of Canal Zone Panamanian authorities to prevent the BSL from landing ships in Panama.[19] Many protesters threatened to strike and burn down the city of Colón if the Panamanian authorities did not yield to the UNIA.

In general, Garvey stood between radical movements and the black masses. He refused to have anything to do with socialism or communism because he considered these movements to be inherently prejudiced against black workers, due to their white leadership. At the same time, he saw no reason not to collaborate with "certain types of radicals," usually those involved in "anti-colonial, anti-imperialist or antiracist struggles."[20] Garvey complimented leaders like Vladimir Lenin and Leon Trotsky, whose desire to achieve a better life for their people resembled his own. He also expressed great respect for A. A. Cipriani, a white leader of the Trinidad Workingmen's Association (TWA), with whom he shared many political views. Black members of the TWA encouraged Cipriani's nomination as leader of the trade union in 1919. According to one scholar, "By this time the association had already become a Garveyite stronghold in Trinidad and its struggles were being reported in the *Negro World*."[21]

In December 1919 Trinidadian dockworkers from both the TWA and the UNIA effectively shut down all commerce in Port-of-Spain, insisting that British officials meet their demands for higher wages and improved working conditions. The strike then spread to rural workers in Tobago. Violent protests involving Jamaican-born veterans of World War I erupted in Jamaica, Grenada, Panama, Belize, and other parts of the Caribbean around the same time as the 1919 strike in Trinidad. In Belize's capital city, the UNIA played a central role in a protest against merchant price hikes in July 1919. Ex-Sergeant Samuel Haynes, secretary of the UNIA in Belize, served as one of the principal leaders of a large race-conscious labor revolt in the capital. The demonstrations sent British colonial officials scrambling to regain control over the city. Working-class grievances centered on high merchant prices for subsistence goods and depressed wages. When British officials in Belize banned the distribution of Garvey's *Negro World*, UNIA members in nearby Mexico and Guatemala smuggled in the paper in even larger quantities than were previously available.[22]

As in Costa Rica and Belize, Garveyites on the Caribbean coast of Guatemala participated in and supported working-class blacks in struggles against white elites; in most of Central America, UNIA members and black laborers for UFCO were almost inseparable. Historically, as we have seen, worker solidarity on UFCO banana plantations in Izabal had not been easy. Black workers from different backgrounds had a difficult time finding common ground. The message of the UNIA helped to repress ethnic differences among black UFCO workers in Izabal.[23]

Barbadian immigrant Clifford Bourne established the first UNIA branch in Guatemala in February 1920. Bourne was most likely elected UNIA commissioner for Guatemala and Belize by UNIA members at the local level, which was typical among Garveyites. UNIA members in Guatemala also elected Bourne president of the local association. At a May 1920 meeting in Puerto Barrios, Martin exhorted those in attendance to financially support the BSL and the NFC, as well as Bourne's travel expenses to an August 1920 UNIA convention in New York. In a speech, L. A. Davis remarked: "As a race, we depend on others too much and too little on ourselves. . . . The new Negro intends to go forward and have confidence in the Universal Negro Improvement Association and the Hon. Marcus Garvey."[24] Over forty new members joined the chapter at the May 1920 meeting, and well-to-do members of the association purchased two hundred shares of stock in the Black Star Line.[25]

As the success of this meeting suggests, the Caribbean coast had enough prosperous blacks by the early 1920s to bankroll the UNIA in Guatemala. For some shrewd, aggressive, and hard-working black immigrants, as we have seen, migration to the Atlantic coast of Guatemala had paid off handsomely. Despite its violent and corrupt government officials, Guatemala had proven an easier place for a black immigrant to become a property or business owner than the Jim Crow South or the British colonial West Indies. In the department of Izabal, black immigrants from the United States and the West Indies became property owners and entrepreneurs. Black-owned restaurants, bars, and jazz clubs generated enough income by the 1920s to make Garveyism viable on the Caribbean coast of Guatemala. The Puerto Barrios chapter of the UNIA sent a thousand dollars to UNIA national headquarters in May 1920. Black migrants went on to establish additional chapters and Liberty Halls in other parts of Guatemala, including the districts of Los Amates, Guatemala City, Morales, and Livingston.[26]

Delegates to the August 1920 UNIA convention, including Bourne, joined in adopting a Declaration of Rights of the Negro Peoples of the World, which included a statement declaring that Africans must struggle to obtain justice using every method possible, that white judges and all-white juries had no authority to try black defendants, and that the taxation of black citizens without representation was unacceptable.[27] In June, UNIA members at the branch in Puerto Barrios had established a union that organized and supported Caribbean coast workers. Bourne reported to the convention on the role that UNIA members in Guatemala had played in the struggle of the UFCO workers (which included IRCA laborers) to "raise the laborers' salary 100 percent." The UNIA in Guatemala had supported worker demands by creating a strike fund that allowed UFCO workers to stay off the job long enough for the company to feel the pain of the work stoppage—which did not take long, given that bananas rot quickly. "We established a charitable fund and everybody held up work for about fifteen days and they came to us and we supported them," Bourne announced to the assembled UNIA delegates. UFCO's white management evidently saw that its black labor force, with the financial and moral support of UNIA, was united, organized, and "determined" to strike until its demands were met. As a result, Bourne reported: "When the white m[a]n saw that we were determined not be led by him, the manager of the company gave the men [a] 100 percent raise. All of that was accomplished through the Universal Negro Improvement Association."[28]

In the summer of 1921 Garvey and other members of the UNIA's executive staff toured the Atlantic coast of Belize and Guatemala. Locals and West Indian immigrants met them with "great enthusiasm." After Belize, Garvey went to Puerto Barrios. "There, too, the natives joined with the West Indians and with a few American Negroes who are down there in joining the U.N.I.A," wrote one of the executive staff members who traveled with Garvey.[29] Garvey intended his message of black uplift and solidarity against racism to be a rallying cry for the support of an autonomous black government and economic system. But in places like Puerto Barrios, black immigrants interpreted Garveyism differently—or possibly co-opted it—to organize black workers against white bosses. Black immigrants in Guatemala used Garvey's analysis of black labor exploitation to unite workers, articulate their demands, and raise funds to support the possibility of a prolonged strike.

Although Garvey never embraced communism, some members of his staff did. *Negro World* editor W. A. Domingo, for example, a socialist and a later member of the black communist organization the African Blood Brotherhood (ABB), used his post on the paper's staff to publish Bolshevik propaganda in 1919. When he learned of Domingo's membership in the ABB, Garvey quickly fired him.[30] Garvey held the view that the ABB "was in reality the advocate of Sovietism, Bolshevism and Radicalism, the paid servant of certain destructive white elements which aimed at exploiting Negroes for their own subservient ends."[31] Yet Garvey's critique of UFCO's treatment of black laborers in Central America and his promotion of black capitalism had a radicalizing effect similar to the message of the ABB. Both the ABB and Garvey criticized exploitative white employers. They parted company in their visions for improving the conditions of black workers: the ABB called for multiethnic socialism; Garveyism called for black capitalism operated within a Pan-African world, with an African metropolis interconnected to a global capitalist system by the BSL and NFC.

Conclusion

The arrival of Garveyism in Guatemala offered evidence that blacks in the Central American republic were prosperous enough to support their own community-wide cultural, political, and economic institutions.[32] Black workers rallied around the UNIA in Guatemala and other parts of the Americas for the same reason: the UNIA (and its auxiliaries) provided an institution whose members could network their resources for the purpose of mutual aid and thus improve socioeconomic conditions. In Guatemala, the UNIA served as a civic, cultural, and a trade union institution. It championed the self-worth of black workers and encouraged black business ownership. After its arrival in the 1920s, the UNIA provided an important institutional infrastructure for black immigrants in an increasingly anti-immigrant nation. Moreover, it gave black workers renewed confidence as they united and mobilized in their struggle against UFCO, the Guatemalan state, and Guatemalan workers who wanted their jobs.

Epilogue

In attempting to narrate the history of the multiethnic labor force on the Caribbean coast of Guatemala in the late nineteenth and early twentieth centuries, I have engaged in a project of piecing together fragmented and often-neglected source materials in order to bring an interesting and largely ignored history to light. That black Americans migrated to Guatemala in the 1880s and 1890s is itself a little-known fact; that they were joined there by migrant laborers from the West Indies and elsewhere, and what happened to them after they arrived, is a story that ought to be remembered, for a number of reasons.

It is a story of interest, first of all, because a substantial number of the migrant black laborers in Guatemala seem to have found opportunities for economic advancement there. At the completion of the lowland railroad projects in 1908, some men moved on to the site of the next economic boom in the circum-Caribbean region, some stayed on as employees of IRCA, and others took jobs with UFCO's Guatemalan division. Some became farmers and entrepreneurs: despite its violent and corrupt government officials, Guatemala proved to be an easier place for a black immigrant to become a property or business owner than the Jim Crow South or the British colonial West Indies.

It is a story of interest, too, because the black proletarians, subsistence farmers, and businessmen who stayed on in Guatemala made an indelible mark on Guatemalan culture, particularly in the Caribbean region, where English became the lingua franca, jazz and reggae became popular forms of musical expression, and jerk chicken and meat patties became part of the local cuisine. A 1914 business report written by one Gerrard Harris gives a good impression of the ethnic impact that black immigrants had on the Caribbean region of Guatemala. Harris describes the region as populated by four thousand UFCO employees, principally "Jamaica[n] and American negroes." His estimate does not take into account the number of former IRCA and UFCO employees who, like Louis McPherson and Simon Shine, became farmers and small business owners. In consumer terms, Harris reported, the region had cultural taste akin to the demands for goods in any big general store in the Mississippi Delta or the Black Belt of Alabama, where there was a similar preponderance of wage-earning black people. The difference was that merchants in Caribbean Guatemala were immigrants of African and Chinese descent.[1]

In the 1930s banana disease in Izabal forced UFCO to relocate its plantations to the Pacific coast of Guatemala, causing a dispersion of some portion of the Caribbean coast's Afro-Guatemalan population to other parts of the country in search of new employment opportunities. Away from the Caribbean coast, Afro-Guatemalans worked largely in the agricultural and service industries. In Guatemala City, black American immigrants who once worked for the railroad were highly prized as cooks. But it was the Caribbean coast that remained most indelibly changed by the influx of migrant workers: politically, the region remained a hotbed for radical labor movements into the 1940s, when black immigrants' descendents participated in a revolutionary movement in 1944. Interestingly, the Caribbean remained virtually untouched during the thirty-six years of civil war that raged from 1960 to 1996 between Guatemala's elite, mestizo-controlled central government and largely Mayan insurgent groups. The majority of the insurgents' movements and the government's counterinsurgency activities took place in the highland departments of the country and in Guatemala City.

The workers who arrived in Guatemala in the late nineteenth century also opened up pathways of immigration that remained in use for several generations. In the post–World War II period, Guatemala experienced another wave of black immigration to the Caribbean region; the 1950 census indicated the presence of 1,530 Belizean-born Guatemalans and 435 Jamaicans. Additional black immigrants from Belize and the West Indies have settled in the Caribbean since the 1950s. Today, Guatemala is the most populous and most ethnically diverse country in Central America, with approximately twelve million inhabitants. Fifty-four percent of the population is mestizo, 44 percent is made up of Native American ethnic groups, and 1–2 percent is Afro-Guatemalan, including people of Garifuna, American, Belizean, and West Indian descent.

Yet the ethnic impact of black immigrant workers on Caribbean Guatemala is much stronger than these numbers suggest. While doing fieldwork in Guatemala in 1995 and 1996, I was amazed at the cultural contrast between Guatemala City, the capital of the country, and Puerto Barrios. The capital is rich in Mayan cultural influences along with mestizo culture. On Sundays (the only day off for most working-class people in Guatemala), displays of mestizo culture are almost unnoticeable in the principal plaza, in front of the National Palace, compared to those of the capital's Mayan ethnic groups. With their distinctive, bright-colored pants, dresses, headwear, and languages, you can see Mayans sitting around in clusters, talking and enjoying their day off with friends and family from back home. As a six-foot-one black American, I towered over the diminutive Mayan immigrants. They seemed equally interested in studying me, as we tried to make sense of our ethnic differences. On the Caribbean coast, by contrast, I was not as curious to the locals (so long as I didn't talk). The majority of locals did not look much different than the West Indian immigrants I have encountered in different parts of Brooklyn, home to New York City's largest West Indian community. When you disembark from the bus in Puerto Barrios, you feel as though you have left the Republic of Guatemala and arrived in small, Spanish Town, Jamaica. You also see West Indian–influenced mestizos playing reggae and speaking English, as well as a lot more people of Chinese descent. Recently, this beautiful, low-key and relaxed area of the mainland Caribbean has begun the process of gentrification, as individual investors and corporate and state developers have been buying up real estate and building luxury homes and resorts. It was largely the labor of African Americans that made the region's development possible.

Beyond its important legacy of cultural transmission and economic development, the story of black immigrant workers in Guatemala is significant because they provided an example of labor militancy that was useful for the struggles of later laborers in Guatemala. Black railroad workers—along with a few white and Latin American coworkers—organized the first industrial strikes in modern Guatemalan history. Black industrial workers served as the forerunners to the modern Guatemalan labor movement, in that they organized the earliest challenges to the state and to IRCA, which was owned by the most powerful multinational corporation in Central America. That most of their efforts to improve their working conditions through labor militancy failed should not distract from our appreciation of their legacy: the struggles of black workers against the company in the late nineteenth and early twentieth century inspired the labor organizing of the 1920s, which laid the foundation for a 1940s labor movement that participated in a general strike to overthrow the authoritarian governments of Jorge Ubico in July 1944 and Juan Federico Ponce Vaides in October 1944.

The railway workers' union, the Union for Action and Improvement of Railroads (Sindicato de Acción y Mejoramiento de Ferrocarriles, or SAMF) had about 4,500 members in the mid-1940s, and according to historian Jim Handy, it was "the best-organized and largest workers' union in the country."[2] SAMF swiftly dominated the Guatemalan labor movement and the Confederation of Guatemalan Workers, formed in October 1944. The October Revolution of 1944 was responsible for the democratic election of Guatemala's first reformist president, Juan José Arévalo Bermejo, who served from March 1945 to March 1951, and who brought his concept of "spiritual socialism" to Guatemala. Arévalo welcomed unions and championed generous labor rights, such as the minimum wage, the eight-hour day, and the six-day work week, as well as the right to organize and the establishment of a labor tribunal to arbitrate disputes. Jacobo Arbenz Guzmán succeeded Arévalo in 1951 in the second democratic election in Guatemala's republican history. Before the CIA orchestrated the overthrow of the left-leaning government of Arbenez in 1954, the SAMF took a very militant position toward IRCA, going on strike in 1944, 1945, 1946, 1947, 1949, and 1950. At the same time, banana plantation workers and dockworkers adopted a similarly belligerent attitude toward UFCO.[3]

The Guatemalan government nationalized the railroad in 1960. Subsequent neglect, irregular traffic, and squatter incursions put the government-owned and operated railroad completely out of business in 1996. As a result, agro-exporters in the coffee and banana industries depended on a costly and environmentally unfriendly highway system to ship goods on the Caribbean coast at Puerto Barrios. In 1997, Henry Posner III's Pittsburgh-based company, the Railroad Development Corporation, gained a fifty-year concession from the Guatemalan government to restore and operate the railroad system. The deal was worth approximately $65 million. By 2005, the old Northern Railroad was up and running again, shipping some 150,000 tons of traffic, but it was having a lot of problems with the government. As for UFCO, financial difficulties forced it to sell its properties in Guatemala to Del Monte in 1972 for $20 million.[4]

The work of historian Deborah Levenson-Estrada on trade-union activity in the 1980s informs us that Guatemala continued to have a very strong labor movement in Guatemala City, despite right-wing governments, and this was also the case in Caribbean Guatemala.[5] Today, all of the banana plantations are unionized. While doing fieldwork in Izabal in 1996, I witnessed a massive militant strike of banana workers against Del Monte, in which workers prevented all traffic (including the bus I was on) from entering the only highway in and out of Puerto Barrios. Another strike against Del Monte occurred in 1999; this time, the company used violence to end worker protests against company rollbacks. The legacy of Guatemalan labor activism, then, is one in which militancy, with its roots in the protests of the Caribbean coastal workers of the late nineteenth century, continued to feed a strong movement throughout the twentieth century: black, and then later, predominately mestizo workers on the coast supported the overthrow of repressive governments in Guatemalan in 1897, 1920, and 1944, and successive military dictatorships in Guatemala since 1954 have not been able to repress labor union activity. The example of these early coastal workers provides an important historical reminder to unionized workers throughout contemporary Guatemala that wealthy, multinational companies and repressive governments can be forced to treat workers with dignity and respect.

Notes

Abbreviations

AGCA	Archivo General de Centro América
ED-FRUS	Executive Documents, Foreign Relations of the United States
exp.	expediente [at the AGCA, refers to a single document]
IAG	Records of the Department of State Relating to the Internal Affairs of Guatemala, 1909–1929
JPAV	Jefatura Política de Alta Verapaz
JPI	Jefatura Política de Izabal
leg.	legajo [at the AGCA, refers to a bundle of documents]
MF	Ministerio de Fomento
MGJ	Ministro de Gobernación y Justicia
MRE	Ministerio de Relaciónes Exteriores
NAB	National Archives and Records Administration, National Archives Building, Washington, DC
NACP	National Archives and Records Administration, College Park, MD
paq.	paquette [at the AGCA, refers to a bundle of documents held together by a piece of twine]
RG24	Record Group 24: Records of the Bureau of Naval Personnel
RG59	Record Group 59: General Records of the Department of State
RG84	Record Group 84: Records of the Foreign Service Posts of the Department of State
RG101	Record Group 101: Records of the Office of the Comptroller of the Currency

Introduction

1. Unless otherwise stated, the term "Latin Americans" is used in this book to mean "mestizos"—Spanish-speaking individuals of mixed Spanish and Amerindian descent. For example, the Garifuna are Latin Americans of African descent who speak their own language in addition to Spanish and English.

2. *El Guatemalteco*, January–December 1884; unless otherwise indicated, all Guatemalan newspapers cited are part of the Collección de Venezuela, Hemeroteca de la Biblioteca Nacional de Guatemala, in Guatemala City. See also Castellano H. B. to Jefe Político de Izabal, 11 January 1921, JPI, paq. 1, no. 157, AGCA.

3. Edward Reed to William P. Kent, 14 May 1909, RG84, vol. 138, NACP.

4. M. F. Friely to Bucklin, 31 March 1911, pp. 1–2, RG59, IAG, box 3835, dispatch no. 187, NACP; "Memorandum to Dr. Rose Regarding Guatemala," p. 1., RC, RG101, series 319, box 31, folder 183, NACP.

5. Gilroy, *The Black Atlantic*, 17, 19, 37; Linebaugh and Rediker, *The Many-Headed Hydra*, 61, 77, 179, 206. Also see Benjamin, Hall, and Rutherford, *The Atlantic World in the Age of Empire*; and Clifford, "Diaspora," 302–38, 320, 321.

6. For studies on labor and the coffee industry in Guatemala, see McCreery, "Coffee and Class," 438–60; McCreery, "Debt Servitude in Rural Guatemala," 735–59; Cambranes, *500 años de lucha por la tierra*; and Smith, *Guatemalan Indians and the State*. The only secondary source that mentions railroad laborers participating in the 1897 revolutionary movement is Lemus, *Monografía del Departamento de Zacapa*, 144–45.

7. Examples of this orthodox view include Kepner, *Social Aspects of the Banana Industry*, 181; García, "El movimimiento obrero en Guatemala, 1900–1954"; Sagastume, "La empresa de los ferrocarriles de Guatemala"; and Balcárcel, "El movimiento obrero en Guatemala," 23. The exception to the orthodox view can be found in Oliva Medina, *Artesanos y obreros costarricenses*.

8. For examples of historians who have overlooked African American workers in Latin America, see Spalding, *Organized Labor in Latin America*; Conniff, *Black Labor on a White Canal*; Gaspar, *Limón, 1880–1940*; Bourgois, *Ethnicity at Work*; Acuña Ortega, *Historia general de Centro América*; Chomsky, *West Indian Workers and the United Fruit Company in Costa Rica*; Gordon, *Disparate Diasporas*; Harpelle, *The West Indians of Costa Rica*; and, most recently, Putnam, *The Company They Kept*. Exceptions to this trend include Kepner, *Social Aspects of the Banana Industry*; Guerra-Borges, "Comunicaciones internas y puertos," 547–58; and, most recently, Brown, *The Panama Canal*. Also see the works of the scholars mentioned in note 19.

9. The most recent contribution to this task is Brock and Fuertes, *Between Race and Empire*.

10. Putnam, *The Company They Kept*, 57.

11. Burns, *The Poverty of Progress*, 86.

12. *El Guatemalteco*, January–December 1884; James F. Sarg, United States Consular Agency, 7 January 1885, RG24, ED-FRUS, vol. 2368, p. 68, NAB; *El Norte*, 7 February 1893, 30 April 1893, 10 June 1893, and 17 June 1893; *El Ferrocarril*, 14 March 1894; Agustin Cordero to Ministerio de la Guerra, 17 October 1893, MRE, leg. 7597, Ferrocarril Norte, pp. 4, 7, AGCA; F. J. E. Ortiz, Dirección del Ferrocarril al Norte, to Ministerio de Fomento, 21 March 1894, Ministerio de Fomento, Superintendencia Ferrocarril Norte 1894, leg. 15811, AGCA; *El Ferrocarril*, 19 April 1894, 23 April 1894, 18 July 1894.

13. William T. Penney, "Notes and Comments on Travels through Mexico and Central America, being the personal happenings to and experiences of yours sincerely, Guatemala City, 1913," 89–91, Latin American Library, Tulane University, Rare

Book and Manuscript Department, New Orleans, Louisiana (hereafter cited as Penney Diary).

14. Stuart Lipton, "Annual Report on Commerce and Industries for 1914," 2 May 1915, RG84, vol. 183, NACP.

15. Petras, *Jamaican Labor Migration*, 101; Putnam, *The Company They Kept*, 56–58, 62.

16. Palma Ramos, "El negro en las relaciones etnicas," 16; Herrera, "The African Slave Trade in Early Santiago," 6; Lokken, "Afro-Indigenous Guatemala"; Lutz, *Santiago de Guatemala*, 83–95; Lutz and Restall, "Wolves and Sheep?"; Lokken, "Undoing Racial Hierarchy," 25–36; Lokken, "From Black to *Ladino*"; Komisaruk, "The Work It Cost Me," 4–24.

17. Euraque, *Reinterpreting the Banana Republic*, chap. 2; Rosenthal, "Controlling the Line," 31, 49–50, 64–165; Bak, "Labor, Community, and the Making of a Cross-Class Alliance in Brazil," 179–227; Schell, *Integral Outsiders*, 24–25; Brown, "Foreign and Native-Born Workers in Porfirian, Mexico," 798; Parlee, "The Impact of the United States Railroad Unions on Organized Labor and Government Policy in Mexico," 446–48; Petras, *Jamaican Labor Migration*, 68–71; Conniff, *Black Labor on a White Canal*, 12–35; Fraginals, Pons, and Engerman, *Between Slavery and Free Labor*, chap. 5; Knight and Palmer, *The Modern Caribbean*, 209–11, 236.

18. Bourgois, *Ethnicity at Work*, 59–61; Gillick, "Life and Labor in a Banana Enclave," 160–61; Harpelle, *The West Indians of Costa Rica*, xvi.

19. This interpretation developed out of mobilization theories put forth in Helg, *Our Rightful Share*, 13–14; Linebaugh and Rediker, *The Many-Headed Hydra*, 179; and Euraque, *Reinterpreting the Banana Republic*, 37.

20. Asociación de Investigación y Estudios Sociales Dirección, *Más de 100 años del movimiento obrero urbano en guatemala*, 332–33; Dosal, *Doing Business with the Dictators*, 129.

21. Rosenthal, "Controlling the Line," 58; Dosal, *Doing Business with the Dictators*, chap. 7.

22. Dosal, *Doing Business with the Dictators*, chap. 6; Asociación de Investigación y Estudios Sociales Dirección, *Más de 100 años del movimiento obrero urbano en guatemala*, 74–77, 84, 91, 105–6; Gillick, "Life and Labor in a Banana Enclave," 202.

Chapter 1. Historical Context: Race and Labor in Guatemala

1. Palma Ramos, "El negro en las relaciones etnicas," 16; Herrera, "The African Slave Trade in Early Santiago," 6; Lokken, "Afro-Indigenous Guatemala," 2002; Lutz, *Santiago de Guatemala*, 83–95; Lutz and Restall; Lokken, "Undoing Racial Hierarchy," 25–36; Lokken, "From Black to *Ladino*"; Komisaruk, "The Work It Cost Me," 4–24.

2. Lutz, *Santiago de Guatemala*, 86; Herrera, "The African Slave Trade in Early

Santiago," 6; Komisaruk, "The Work It Cost Me," 5; Lokken, "From Black to *Ladino*," 10–11, 14; Lokken, "Afro-Indigenous Guatemala," 1–2, 5, 8–9; Lokken, "Undoing Racial Hierarchy," 27; Lutz and Restall, "Wolves and Sheep?," 8, 12.

3. Lokken, "From Black to *Ladino*," 10–11, 14; Lokken, "Afro-Indigenous Guatemala," 1–2, 5, 10; Lokken, "Undoing Racial Hierarchy," 27.

4. Lokken, "Undoing Racial Hierarchy," 27.

5. Lutz and Restall, "Wolves and Sheep?," 193.

6. Herrera, "The African Slave Trade in Early Santiago," 7–9; Lutz and Restall, "Wolves and Sheep?," 14–16.

7. Lokken, "Undoing Racial Hierarchy," 28; Lokken, "From Black to *Ladino*," 13, 16–17, 19–20.

8. Kunst, "Notes on Negroes in Guatemala during the Seventeenth Century," 390–97; Gage, *A New Survey of the West Indies*, 205, 208–9.

9. Gage, *A New Survey of the West Indies*, 208–9.

10. Lokken "A Maroon Moment," 53–54.

11. Lokken, "Afro-Indigenous Guatemala," 10; Lutz and Restall, "Wolves and Sheep?," 197; Rout, *The African Experience in Spanish America*, 261–62; Echeverri-Gent, "Forgotten Workers," 282.

12. J. H. Watts to Fenton R. McCreery, 6 July 1910, RG84, vol. 48, From Consuls, 28 February 1910–30, December 1910, McCreery American Legation, Honduras, NACP.

13. J. H. Watts to Fenton R. McCreery, 19 August 1910, RG84, vol. 48, From Consuls, 28 February 1910–30 December 1910, McCreery American Legation, Honduras, NACP.

14. Opie, "Adios Jim Crow," 22–23.

15. Ross, *Development of Railroads in Guatemala and El Salvador*, 33.

16. Dosal, *Doing Business with the Dictators*, 17, 18, 24.

17. Opie, "Adios Jim Crow," 24–25.

18. Chapman, *Jungle Capitalists*, 54–55; Dosal, *Doing Business with the Dictators*, 17, 18, 24.

19. Gudmundson and Lindo-Fuentes, *Central America, 1821–1871*, 87, 127.

20. Ibid., 127.

21. Ibid., 87, 88, 127.

22. Asociación de Investigación y Estudios Sociales Dirección, *Más de 100 años del movimiento obrero urbano en guatemala*, 15–19, 27–28, 31.

23. Crisanto Meléndez and Savaranga, *Adeija sisira gererun aguburigu garinagu*, 15–20; Brigham, *Guatemala*, 29, 37–38.

24. Frank C. Dennis to M. J. Bynum, 2 December 1902, RG84, General and Official Correspondence, 24 March 1902–15 February 1904, vol. 10, p. 196, NACP.

25. Ross, *Development of Railroads in Guatemala and El Salvador*, 33.

26. See Whitehouse to James B. Porter, 24 May 1885, plus enclosures (an article from *El Guatemalteco* on decree no. 330 and a map showing the district opened for colonization by the decree of 15 May 1885), RG59, roll 5, no. 41, pp. 1–7, NACP.

27. Florentin Souza to President Manuel Estrada Cabrera, 20 October 1904, "El importante problem de colonizar la riquisa zona que had dado ser atravesada por rieles y locomotores," MF, leg. B106-1, AGCA; H. Remsen Whitehouse to James B. Porter, 24 May 1885, RG59, Dispatches from United States Consuls in Guatemala, 1824–1906, micro copy no. T-337, roll 5, no. 41, pp. 1–7, NACP.

28. Bella and Byron Tunnell to unknown family in the United States, 1 March 1895, 15 March 1895, Tunnell Family, Letters, 1894-95, Cornell University Library, Special Collections, Ithaca, NY; Bucklin to Secretary of State, 17 October 1910, RG59, IAG, box 3835, dispatch no. 22, pp. 1–2, NACP.

29. Bella and Byron Tunnell to unknown family, 1 March 1895, 15 March 1895, Tunnell Family, Letters, 1894-95, Cornell University Library, Special Collections, Ithaca, NY; Bucklin to Secretary of State, 17 October 1910, RG59, IAG, box 3835, dispatch no. 22, pp. 1–2, NACP.

30. Mack, *The Land Divided*, 338–39.

31. *British Documents on Foreign Affairs—Reports and Papers from the Foreign Office Confidential Print*, 7:128, 251.

32. Ibid., 7:131, 261.

33. Petras, *Jamaican Labor Migration*, 101; Knight and Palmer, *The Modern Caribbean*, 211. Others migrated to the sugarcane plantations of Cuba and the Dominican Republic; North Americans controlled these industries as well.

34. Reproduction of a 5 January 1896 letter from F. García, Superintendent del Ferrocarril al Norte, to the Minister of Development, 14 January 1896, MF, Ferrocarril al Norte, leg. 15815, pp. 16–17, AGCA.

35. Ibid.

36. Contracto: Para conservacion y exploitación de los cincos primeros tramos del Ferrocarril del Norte entre "Puerto Barrios" y "el Rancho de San Agustin" y para la reposición de durmientes entre los estaciónes de "Tenedores" y "La Iguana," pp. 8, 9, 12, MF, Ferrocarril al Norte, leg. 15817, AGCA.

37. Ibid.

38. Contracto: para conservacion y exploitación de los cincos primeros tramos del Ferrocarril del Norte entre Puerto Barrios y el Rancho de San Agustín y para la reposición de durmientes entre los estaciónes de Tenedores ye La Iguana," pp. 8, 9, 12, MF, Ferrocarril al Norte, leg. 15817, AGCA.

39. F. G. Williamson to Leslie Combs, 30 January 1905, RG84, Miscellaneous letters received 1905 American Consulate General Guatemala, Gualan, vol. 91, NACP.

40. *El Norte*, 20 April 1893.

41. Filberto de Leon to the Minister of Development, 24 June 1896, MF, Ferrocarril Vera Paz, leg. 15864, AGCA; *El Norte*, 20 April 1893.

42. Petras, *Jamaican Labor Migration*, 68, 69, 89.

43. Ibid., 49–52, 71, 96; Knight and Palmer, *The Modern Caribbean*, 236.

44. Haskin, *The Panama Canal*, 156–57.

45. Ibid.

46. *El Norte*, 17 June 1893.

47. The names of these U.S. regions come from documents used sporadically by consular officials to document U.S. citizens living in Guatemala; they were found in the U.S. Consular and State Department records on Guatemala, RG84, NACP.

48. Arnesen, *Brotherhoods of Color*, 10.

49. Dailey, Gilmore, and Simon, *Jumpin' Jim Crow*, 142–43; Arnesen, *Waterfront Workers of New Orleans*, 68; Arnesen, "Like Banquo's Ghost, It Will Not Down," 1607. See also Shugg, *Origins of Class Struggle in Louisiana*, 251–52, 297, and Letwin, *The Challenge of Interracial Unionism*, 141–42, 145.

50. Dailey, Gilmore, and Simon, *Jumpin' Jim Crow*, 140, 147.

51. *Weekly Louisianan* (New Orleans), 8 January 1881.

52. *Weekly Louisianan* (New Orleans), 23 April 1881.

53. Alfred A. Winslow to Francis B. Loomis, 6 December 1904, RG84, vol.12, pp. 213–19, NACP.

54. Reed to William P. Kent, 23 February 1909, RG84, vol. 138, p. 221, NACP.

55. Penney Diary, 155.

56. Wm. Rockwill to D. Lynch Pringle, 12 January 1897, RG84, vol. 26, NACP.

57. Dennis to Beaupré, 29 October 1898, RG84, vol. 76, pp. 1–3, NACP.

58. Thomas Perry and John Green to President William McKinley, 25 August 1898, RG84, vol. 27, NACP.

59. Affidavits of George Walters, 16 September 1907, Sam Lee, 16 September 1907, and Simon Shine, 20 September 1907, all in RG84, vol. 40, NACP; dispatches from Reed to Kent, 10 October 1908, RG84, vol. 40, p. 2, NACP.

60. Affidavit of George Martin, 14–16 October 1914, RG84, vol. 176, pp. 1–3; affidavit of Louis McPherson, 21 June 1921, RG84, vol. 209, NACP.

61. Reed to Owen, 20 January 1910, RG84, vol. 140; Correspondence, Consular Agency, American Consulate General, 1910–1911, RG84, vol. 184, enclosure no. 1., p. 17, NACP.

62. Reed to Winslow, 23 May 1903, RG84, vol. 39; Ira L. Penix to Lipton, 20 October 1915, RG84, vol. 182; Jay McCall to Lipton, 3 November 1915, RG84, vol. 182, NACP.

63. Edward Reed to William Owen, 20 October 1913, RG84, vol. 170, pp. 1–3, Correspondence, American Consulate, Guatemala City, 1913, part 3, NACP; Victor Onora to Alberto S. Quiñoes, 4 August 1913, pp. 1–2, JPI, AGCA; "Criminal contra Santiago W. Levy alias Dessert por los delitos de robo y lesions," no. 20, 1913, JPI, 1912, paq. 5, AGCA.

64. Owen, "List of American Citizens Residing in Guatemala, 23 August 1915, enclosure no. 1, dispatch no. 128, RG84, vol. 184, p. 29, NACP; Reed to Owen, 20 October 1913, RG84, vol. 170, pp. 1–3, NACP; Onora to Quiñoes, 4 August 1913, pp. 1–2, AGCA; Quiñoes, 22 August 1913, pp. 1–2, AGCA.

65. Onora to Quiñoes, 4 August 1913, Puerto Barrios, pp. 1–2, AGCA.

66. Sub-general de International Railroad of Central America to Juez de la Instancia, 14 September 1913, "Criminal," 1913, p. 51, NACP.

67. Policía Urbana to Juez de Paz Izabal, 15 August 1913, "Criminal," 1913, p. 32, AGCA.

68. Quiñoes to Juez Municipal, 22 August 1913, "Criminal," pp. 1–2, AGCA.

69. Reed to Owen, 20 October 1913, RG84, vol. 170, pp. 1–3, NACP.

70. Winston James shows this to have been the case among West Indian workers; see his *Holding Aloft the Banner of Ethiopia*, 70.

71. Letwin, *The Challenge of Interracial Unionism*, 118, 120–21.

72. Arnesen, *Brotherhoods of Color*, 33–34.

73. Arnesen, *Waterfront Workers of New Orleans*, 91–92.

74. *Weekly Louisianan* (New Orleans), 3 April 1880, 1 May 1880; *Times Democrat* article republished in the Louisianan.

75. Dailey, *Before Jim Crow*, 11; Conniff, *Black Labor on a White Canal*, 26; Arnesen, *Waterfront Workers of New Orleans*, 92, 114; Kelly, *Race, Class, and Power*, 114; Letwin, *The Challenge of Interracial Unionism*, 147.

76. Petras, *Jamaican Labor Migration*, 63.

77. Ibid., 89–90; Mack, *The Land Divided*, 541; Conniff, *Black Labor on a White Canal*, 26.

78. Arnesen, *Brotherhoods of Color*, 30–31; Arnesen, "Like Banquo's Ghost, It Will Not Down," 1610.

79. Winter, *Guatemala and Her People of Today*, 147–48; Ruhl, *The Central Americans*, 222–23.

80. Arnesen, *Waterfront Workers of New Orleans*, 120–21.

81. Shugg, *Origins of Class Struggle in Louisiana*, 292–93, 297–98.

82. Ibid.

83. Letwin, *The Challenge of Interracial Unionism*, 112, 141.

84. Ibid.

Chapter 2. Race, Resistance, and Revolution in the Late Nineteenth Century

1. McCreery, "Coffee and Class," 451.

2. Third Assistant Secretary of the Department of State, Washington, D.C., to D. Lynch Pringle, 2 June 1897, original enclosure, RG84, vol. 26, NACP.

3. Dennis to Pringle, 6 February 1897, dispatch no. 186, pp. 2, 4–6, 8–12, 14, 16, RG84, vol. 72, NACP.

4. James F. Sarg, 7 January 1885, RG24, ED-FRUS, vol. 2368, p. 68, NAB.

5. Dennis to Vice Consul General J. N Todd, 4 February 1896, RG84, vol. 71, NACP.

6. Owen to Dennis, 10 February 1897, RG84, vol. 93, pp. 1–2; *Cincinnati Enquirer*, RG84, vol. 26, NACP.

7. Brigham, *Guatemala*, 29, 37–38.

8. García to Ministerio de Fomento, 24 November 1894, MF, leg. 15812, no. 274, AGCA; Davis, *Three Gringos in Venezuela and Central America*, 25, 26.

9. García to Minister of Development, 14 January 1896, MF, Ferrocarril al Norte,

leg. 15815, pp. 16–17, AGCA; "queja de los subditos británicos Alfred Morgan y Silvestre Esparks contra el Juez de Zacapa," January 1896, transcription of a 3 February 1896 letter from F. James J. Roberts of the British Legation to the Ministro de Relaciones Exteriores, MGJ, leg. 28912, exp. 133, pp. 9–10, AGCA.

10. Winter, *Guatemala and Her People of Today*, 146.

11. Asturias, *Strong Wind*, 30. In addition to the diversity of languages, another interesting aspect about Izabal is the fact that until the 1920s it was the least populated department in Guatemala, with the smallest population of Mayan ethnic groups (see Carillo Ramírez, *Tierras de Oriente*, 129).

12. Jose M. Amerlinck to García, 4 December 1895, MF, leg. 15813, AGCA.

13. Reed to Kent, 24 October 1908, RG84, vol. 40, pp. 1–3, NACP; Owen to Dennis, 10 February 1897, RG84, vol. 93, pp. 1–2, NACP.

14. Jones, Scoullar, and Hall, *El "Libro azul" de Guatemala*, 134.

15. Penney Diary, 112, 134, 138, 141; Martin Roberts and A. C. Ham to Mr. Rafael Spinola, 21 July 1900, MF, leg. B106-1, p. 7, AGCA; de Villeda Mainieri, "Algunos aspectos de la economía de Guatemala de 1892 a 1898," 55.

16. Amerlinck to García, 27 March 1897, MF, leg. 15817, AGCA; L. P. Pennypacker to Amerlinck, 11 November 1897, leg. 15819, pp. 100–103, AGCA.

17. Penney Diary, 65, 89, 90, 91, 112, 134, 138, 141.

18. McCreery, "Debt Servitude in Rural Guatemala," 744, 747.

19. Sarg to Whitehouse, 5 December 1884, RG84, vol. 26, p. 67, NAB; Sarg to Whitehouse, 28 January 1885, RG84, vol. 26, pp. 69–70, NAB; Sarg to Whitehouse, 28 January 1885, RG24, ED-FRUS, vol. 2368, NAB; *Cincinnati Enquirer* article of June 1897, found in RG84, vol. 26, NACP.

20. Penney Diary, 155; Anni L. Chubb to State Department, 11 July 1911, RG84, vol. 82, pp. 1–2, NACP; R. K. Thomas, 3–19 February 1923, RG59, roll 20, pp. 368–73, NACP.

21. UFCO passenger list, JPI, 1921, paq. 4, AGCA.

22. American citizenship registration record dated 3 October 1912, RG84, vol. 167, NACP.

23. Cunningham, *Gypsying through Central America*, 237; Reed to Kent, 23 February 1909, RG84, vol. 138, p. 221, NACP; Henry Collins, 25 January 1909, RG84, vol. 40, NACP.

24. *El Norte*, 20 April 1893; Amerlinck to García, 4 December 1895, MF, leg. 15813, AGCA.

25. Penney Diary, 68; Pennypacker to Amerlinck, 11 November 1897, MF, leg. 15819, pp. 100–103, AGCA; R. H. May and Pennybacker to Amerlinck, 21 September 1898, MF, leg. 15821, p. 1, AGCA.

26. Affidavit of George Martin, 14–16 October 1914, RG84, vol. 176, pp. 1–3, NACP.

27. Amerlinck to García, 4 December 1895, MF, leg. 15813, AGCA; Juzgado de 1a Instancia, Department of Zacapa, to Ministerio de Gobernación y Justicia, 4 Febru-

ary 1897, MGJ, leg. 28935, pp. 1–2, AGCA; Wm. F. Fugua to Pringle, 19 June 1897, RG84, vol. 93, NACP.

28. Elias Estrada to Ministerio de Gobernación y Justicia, 2 February 1897, MGJ, leg. 28935, pp. 1–2; Juzgado de 1a Instancia del Dept de Zacapa to Ministerio de Gobernación y Justicia, 4 February 1897, MGJ, leg. 28935, pp. 1–2, AGCA.

29. Elias Estrada to Ministerio de Gobernación y Justicia, 2 February 1897, MGJ, leg. 28935, pp. 1–2; Juzgado de 1a Instancia del Dept de Zacapa to Ministerio de Gobernación y Justicia, 4 February 1897, MGJ, leg. 28935, pp. 1–2, AGCA; Collin C. W. Owen to Dennis, 10 February 1897, RG84, vol. 93, pp. 1–2, NACP.

30. Whitehouse to Porter, 24 May 1885, RG59, roll 5, no. 41, pp. 1–7, NACP.

31. Dennis to Pringle, 6 February 1897, RG84, vol. 72, dispatch no. 186, pp. 2, 4–6, 8–12, 14, 16, NACP.

32. *Cincinnati Enquirer* article of June 1897, found in RG84, vol. 26, NACP.

33. John Claude Watts to His Parents, 20 November 1896, RG84, vol. 25, NACP.

34. Brigham, *Guatemala*, 62; Bucklin to Howard, 12 September 1911, RG84, vol. 154, NACP.

35. Penney Diary, 135, 151.

36. Henry C. Hall to Fred'k T. Frelinghuysen, 15 January 1885, RG24, ED-FRUS, vol. 2368, p. 66, NAB.

37. *Cincinnati Enquirer* article of June 1897, found in RG84, vol. 26, NACP; Penney Diary, 65.

38. Con Hickey to Consular Guatemala City, 24 December 1885, RG59, micro copy no. T-337, roll 5, enclosure no. 33, pp. 1–2, NACP.

39. Sarg to Whitehouse, 5 December 1884, p. 67, and 28 January 1885, RG24, ED-FRUS, vol. 2368, pp. 69–70, NAB.

40. Sarg to Whitehouse, 5 December 1884, RG24, ED-FRUS, vol. 2368, p. 67, NAB; Sarg to Whitehouse, 28 January 1885, RG24, ED-FRUS, vol. 2368, pp. 69–70, NAB.

41. Sarg to Whitehouse, 28 January 1885, RG24, ED-FRUS, vol. 2368, p. 69, NAB.

42. Ibid., p. 6.

43. Ibid., p. 72; Frelinghuysen to Hall, 27 February 1885, RG24, ED-FRUS, vol. 2368, NAB; log book entries of J. C. Wiltse, U.S. Navy Commander, USS *Swatara*, for 10 September 1884 through 17 March 1885, and 27 March 1885, RG24, ED-FRUS, vol. 2368, NAB.

44. Sarg to Whitehouse, 17 March 1885, 19 March 1885, 27 March 1885, RG24, ED-FRUS, vol. 2368, pp. 90–91, NAB.

45. Log book entries of J. C. Wiltse, U.S. Navy Commander, USS *Swatara*, for 17 March 1885, 19 March 1885, 27 March 1885, RG24, ED-FRUS, vol. 2368, NAB.

46. F. G. Williamson to Combs, 30 January 1905, RG84, vol. 91, NACP.

47. Penney Diary, 66, 67; Amerlinck to García, 4 December 1895, MF, leg. 15813, AGCA.

48. Jose M. Amerlinck to F. García, 4 December 1895, leg. 15813, MF, AGCA.

49. Toussaint, *Guatemala*, 183–93.

50. May to Arthur Beaupré, 5 October 1898, RG84, vol. 94, p. 2, NACP.

51. According to the *Diario Centro-America*'s 22 September 1897 edition, Fuentes and Morales were of "negro heritage."

52. de Villeda Mainieri, "Algunos aspectos de la economía de Guatemala de 1892 a 1898," 20–22, 57; Lemus, *Monografía del Departamento de Zacapa*, 144–45.

53. Amerlinck to García, 27 March 1897, MF, leg. 15817, AGCA.

54. de Villeda Mainieri, "Algunos aspectos de la economía de Guatemala de 1892 a 1898," 20–22.

55. Ibid.

56. *La Voz del Obrero*, 23 April 1898.

57. *La Voz del Obrero*, 23 April 1898, 20–22; Lemus, *Monografía del Departamento de Zacapa*, 144–45.

58. Jeromino Puiz to Jefe Político de Alta Verapas, 15 October 1897, JPAV, paq. 1, AGCA; C. Bentham to Thos W. Cridler, 8 December 1897, RG84, vol. 27, NACP.

59. *La Voz del Obrero*, 12 May 1898.

60. Dennis to Pringle, 5 November 1897, RG84, vol. 72, dispatch no. 230, pp. 5–9, NACP.

61. Dennis to Pringle, 5 November 1897, RG84, vol. 72, dispatch no. 230, pp. 5–9, NACP.

62. Dennis to Pringle, 5 November 1897, RG84, vol. 72, dispatch no. 230, pp. 5–9, NACP., Dennis to Pringle, 5 November 1897; RG84, vol. 72, dispatch no. 231, pp. 1–3, NACP; Lemus, *Monografía del Departamento de Zacapa*, 144–45.

63. Dennis to Pringle, 5 November 1897, RG84, vol. 72, dispatch no. 231, pp. 1–3, NACP.

64. D. Lynch to Pringle, 13 November 1897, RG84, vol. 37, p. 187, NACP; Elias Estrada Zacapa to Secretary of War, in a 30 November 1897 letter from Grego Solares to Ministro de Relaciónes Exteriores, 25 November 1897, MRE, leg. 9341, AGCA.

65. de Villeda Mainieri, "Algunos aspectos de la economía de Guatemala de 1892 a 1898," 20–22.

66. Ibid.

67. Juan Paz Tomas to Ministro de Gobernación y Justicia, 11 July 1898, MGJ, leg. 28964, exp. 1787, AGCA.

68. Juan Paz Tomas to Ministro de Gobernación y Justicia, 11 July 1898, MGJ, leg. 28964, exp. 1787, AGCA.

69. Dennis to Beaupré, 2 September 1898, RG84, vol. 76, dispatch no. 336, pp. 2, 6, NACP.

70. L. P. Pennybacker to Director Ferrocarril del Norte, 21–22 September 1898, MF, Ferrocarril del Norte, leg. 15822, pp. 191–92, AGCA.

71. L. P. Pennybacker to Minister of Development, 1 October 1898, MF, Ferrocarril del Norte 1898, Telegrams May, leg. 15821, p. 15, AGCA.

72. May to Beaupre, 5 October 1898, RG84, vol. 94, p. 2, NACP.

73. Affidavit of V. Enancio DeLeon, 13 October 1898, "Diligencias Seguidas en relacion a la huelga de los empleados del Ferrocarril del Norte y conducta observada por el ex contratista de esa obra, Igen Robert H. May 1898," MRE, leg. 7597, pp. 8–9; Beaupre to H. C. Park, 24 October 1898, RG84, vol. 94, NACP.

74. Affidavit of V. Enancio DeLeon, 13 October 1898, "Diligencias Seguidas en relacion a la huelga de los empleados del Ferrocarril del Norte y conducta observada por el ex contratista de esa obra, Igen Robert H. May 1898," MRE, leg. 7597, pp. 8–9; Beaupre to H. C. Park, 24 October 1898, RG84, vol. 94, NACP.

75. May to Beaupre, 24 November 1898, RG84, vol. 94, pp. 1–2, NACP.

76. Reed to McNally, 6 December 1900, RG84, vol. 79, dispatch no. 182, pp. 1, 2, 4, 8, NACP.

77. A. Lenersisy, Superintendent to Minister of Development, 10 September 1900, MF, leg. B106-1, pp. 1, 2, AGCA; Pennypacker to Ministro de Fomento, "Presupuesto de Oficina del Director General, Dirección General de Obras Publicas," 4 May 1900, MF, leg. B106-1, p. 2, AGCA.

Chapter 3. Race Relations on the Early-Twentieth-Century Caribbean Frontier

1. Hugh R. Wilson to Secretary of State, 21 October 1912, RG59, IAG, box 3838, NACP; Garrard Harris, 1914, RG84, vol. 179, NACP.

2. Lipton to Harris, 19 January 1915, RG84, vol. 183, NACP.

3. Bourgois, *Ethnicity at Work*, 62.

4. Williams, "The Rise of the Banana Industry," 118.

5. Affidavits of George Walters, 16 September 1907, and Simon Shine, 20 September 1907, RG84, vol. 40, NACP; affidavit of Simon Shine, 13 November 1907, RG84, vol. 122, pp. 201-2, NACP; Reed to Kent, 22 September 1907, RG84, vol. 122, pp. 263–68, NACP.

6. Affidavits of George Walters, 16 September 1907, and Simon Shine, 20 September 1907, RG84, vol. 40, NACP; affidavit of Simon Shine, 13 November 1907, RG84, vol. 122, pp. 201-2, NACP; Reed to Kent, 22 September 1907, RG84, vol. 122, pp. 263–68, NACP; Edward Reed to William Owen, 20 January 1910, RG84, vol. 140, AGCA.

7. Lionel Carden to Juan Barrios M., 19 March 1908, MRE, leg. 8562, pp. 1–2, AGCA.

8. Dosal, *Doing Business with the Dictators*, 40–41. For more on Keith, see Stewart, *Keith and Costa Rica*, chaps. 1–6; Acuña Ortega, *Historia general de Centro América*.

9. Ministerio de Fomento, "Certificacion Del Los Contractos Celebrados Para La Conclusion y Explotacion Del 'Ferrocarril Del Norte,' Y Derechos de Aprobacion," 1901, leg. B106-1, p. 3, AGCA.

10. Reed to Hunter, 1 June 1901, RG84, vol. 18, dispatch no. 84, p. 3, NACP; Bar-

thel to Ministerio de Fomento, 16 July 1901 and 2 August 1901, MF, leg. B106-1, AGCA.

11. Barthel to Ministerio de Fomento, 5 October 1901, MF, leg. B106-1, AGCA.

12. Ibid.

13. William Balz, 13 May 1911, RG84, vol. 176, pp. 80–88, NACP.

14. Putnam, *The Company They Kept*, 174; Gillick, "Life and Labor in a Banana Enclave," 89.

15. Affidavit de Oscar Bell Payne, RG84, vol. 147, pp. 61–62, NACP; Oscar Bell Payne to American Consulate General, 12 April 1908, Guatemala, RG84, vol. 147, NACP.

16. Reed to William Owen, 31 August 1909, RG84, vol. 138, NACP.

17. Smith to Sands, 20 December 1909, RG59, IAG, box 3838, dispatch no. 90, pp. 1–5, NACP; Juzgado Municipal de Puerto Barrios to Jefatura Política de Izabal, September 1913, JPI, AGCA.

18. Juzgado Municipal de Puerto Barrios to Jefatura Política de Izabal, September 1913, JPI, AGCA.

19. Affidavit of James Wilson, 11 May 1910, RG84, vol. 153, NACP; P. L. Moore to Edward Reed, 21 August 1913, RG84, vol. 171, NACP.

20. Cunningham, *Gypsying through Central America*, 237.

21. Ibid., 240.

22. Reed to Bucklin, 5 May 1912, RG84, vol. 161, pp. 42–43, NACP.

23. Reed to Bucklin, 5 May 1912, RG84, vol. 161, pp. 6–7, NACP; "Testimonio de Owen H. Hughes," 12 May 1914, MRE, leg. 8567, "Las desordenes ocurido en 'Quiche' y 'Tehuana' distrito de Quirigua, en los cuales hubo varios muertos," pp. 6–7, AGCA; "Testimonio de Lorenzo Flores," 12 May 1914, MRE, leg. 8567, "Las desordenes ocurido en 'Quiche' y 'Tehuana' distrito de Quirigua, en los cuales hubo varios muertos," pp. 8–9, AGCA.

24. Roger P. Ames to Owen, May 17, 1914, RG84, vol. 179, pp. 1–2, NACP.

25. Felipe Morales to Estrada Cabrera, 11 May 1914, MRE, leg. 8567, AGCA.

26. Felipe Morales to Estrada Cabrera, 11 May 1914, MRE, leg. 8567, AGCA; Estrada Cabrera to Jefe Politico de Izabal, 11 May 1914, MRE, leg. 8567, p. 1, AGCA.

27. González Davison, Fernando. *El régimen liberal en Guatemala*, 34, 38–39.

28. Estrada Cabrera to Jefe Politico de Izabal, 11 May 1914, MRE, leg. 8567, p. 1, AGCA.

29. Roger P. Ames to Owen, 17 May 1914, RG84, vol. 179, pp. 1–2, NACP.

30. Roger P. Ames to Owen, 17 May 1914, RG84, vol. 179, pp. 1–2, NACP; Williams, "The Rise of the Banana Industry," 117–18; "Testimonio de Rita Flores," 12 May 1914, MRE, leg. 8567, p. 11, AGCA.

31. "Testimonio de Carmen Villagran y varios Ladinos," 12 May 1914, MRE, leg. 8567, "Las desordenes ocurido en 'Quiche' y 'Tehuana' distrito de Quirigua, en los cuales hubo varios muertos," p. 4, AGCA.

32. Leawell to Secretary of State, 19 May 1914, RG59, IAG, box 3838, dispatch no. 55, pp. 1–2, NACP.

33. "Testimonio de Jorge Ferguson G. y varios Ladinos," 12 May 1914, MRE, leg. 8567, "Las desordenes," pp. 2–3, AGCA.

34. "Testimonio de Jorge Ferguson G. y various Ladinos," 12 May 1914, MRE, leg. 8567, "Las desordenes ocurido en 'Quiche' y 'Tehuana' distrito de Quirigua, en los cuales hubo varios muertos," " pp. 2–3, AGCA; "Testimonio de Lorenzo Flores," 12 May 1914, MRE, leg. 8567, "Las desordenes ocurido en 'Quiche' y 'Tehuana' distrito de Quirigua, en los cuales hubo varios muertos," pp. 8–9, AGCA.

35. Estrada Cabrera, 23 October 1914, RG84, vol. 180, NACP.

36. Gillick, "Life and Labor in a Banana Enclave," 177–79.

37. Lipton to Harris, 19 January 1915, RG84, vol. 183, pp. 26–27, 35–36, NACP; *Censo general de la República de Guatemala . . . 1893; Censo general de la población de la República de Guatemala . . . 1921.*

38. Herbert S. Gold to Minister for Foreign Relations Luis P. Aguirre Migrants, 2 December 1920, MRE, leg. 8535, p. 1, AGCA.

39. Secretaria de Gobernación y Justicia to Jefe Político de Izabal, Jefatura Transcribo, 18 October 1921, JPI, 1921, paq. 1, AGCA.

40. Putnam, *The Company They Kept,* 41.

41. Ibid.

42. Arthur C. Frost, 12 July 1921, Guatemala City, RG84, vol. 211, pp. 1, 3–5, 7, NACP.

Chapter 4. Revolvers, Shotguns, Machetes, and Clubs

1. Smith to Sands, 20 December 1909, RG59, IAG, box 3838, dispatch no. 90, pp. 1–5, NACP.

2. Smith to Sands, 20 December 1909, RG59, IAG, box 3838, dispatch no. 90, pp. 1–5, NACP.

3. Kepner, *Social Aspects of the Banana Industry,* 180–81, 197, 199; Bourgois, *Ethnicity at Work,* 260.

4. Gillick, "Life and Labor in a Banana Enclave," 160–62, 188–89.

5. Ibid.; Harpelle, *The West Indians of Costa Rica.*

6. Other examples of this orthodox view of Guatemalan labor include Asociación de Investigación y Estudios Sociales Dirección, *Más de 100 años del movimiento obrero urbano en guatemala,* 130–33; Balcárcel, "El movimiento obrero en Guatemala," 23; Sagastume, "La empresa de los ferrocarriles de Guatemala," 8, 9; García, "El movimiento obrero en Guatemala, 1900–1954," 15–19. The exception to this trend is González Davison, *El régimen liberal en Guatemala,* 41.

7. Helg, *Our Rightful Share,* 13–14; Forster, "Reforging National Revolution," 202–3.

8. Rodney, *A History of the Guyanese Working People*, 26.

9. Williams, "The Rise of the Banana Industry," 117–19.

10. Ibid., 118–20.

11. Ibid., 120–21.

12. Smith to Sands, 20 December 1909, pp. 1–5; Godfrey Haggard to Luis Estrada Monzon, 23 December 1909, both in Correspondencia a Jefe Politico y Comandante de Armas de Departamento de Izabal, "Documentos relativos a la huelga de jamaiquenos 1909/10 No. 11," JPI, 1910, AGCA.

13. Felipe Estrada Paniagua to Sands, 1 April 1910, RG59, IAG, box 3838, NACP.

14. Smith to Sands, 20 December 1909, RG59, IAG, box 3838, dispatch no. 90, pp. 1–5, NACP.

15. Ibid.

16. Ibid.

17. Ibid.

18. Smith to Sands, 17 December 1909, RG59, IAG, box 3838, dispatch no. 90, pp. 1–5, NACP; Smith to Nicolas Ferguson, 22 December 1909, RG84, vol. 138, "Documentos relativos a la huelga de jamaiquenos," NACP; Reed to Owen, 23 December 1909, RG84, vol. 138, NACP.

19. Smith to Sands, 17 December 1909, RG59, IAG, box 3838, dispatch no. 90, NACP; Warren W. Smith to Nicolas Ferguson, 22 December 1909, RG84, vol. 138, "Documentos relativos a la huelga de jamaiquenos"; Reed to Owen, 23 December 1909, RG84, vol. 138, NACP.

20. Reed to Monzon, 23 December 1909, RG59, IAG, box 3838, NACP.

21. Haggard to Jefe Politico, 23 December 1909, RG84, vol. 138, "Documentos relativos a la huelga de jamaiquenos"; Smith to Sands, 25 December 1909, RG59, IAG, box 3838, NACP.

22. Haggard to Jefe Politico, 23 December 1909, RG84, vol. 138, "Documentos relativos a la huelga de jamaiquenos"; Smith to Sands, 25 December 1909, RG59, IAG, box 3838, NACP.

23. Smith and Ricardo Car Baneda to Monzon, 4 January 1910, JPI, "Documentos relativos a la huelga de jamaiquenos 1909/10 No. 11," AGCA; Smith to Sands, 5 January 1910, RG59, IAG, box 3838, dispatch no. 90, pp. 1–2, NACP; Ricardo Castanado to Monzon, 5 January 1910, JPI, "Documentos relativos a la huelga de jamaiquenos 1909/10 No. 11," AGCA.

24. Smith and Ricardo Car Baneda to Monzon, JPI, "Documentos relativos a la huelga de jamaiquenos 1909/10 No. 11," AGCA; Smith to Sands, 5 January 1910, RG59, IAG, box 3838, dispatch no. 90, pp. 1–2, NACP; Ricardo Castanado to Monzon, 5 January 1910, JPI, "Documentos relativos a la huelga de jamaiquenos 1909/10 No. 11," AGCA.

25. Cutter to Sands, 18 March 1910, RG59, IAG, box 3838, dispatch no. 100, pp. 1–2, NACP; Sands to Secretary of State, 2 April 1910, RG59, IAG, box 3838, NACP;

Wilson to Secretary of State, 17 June 1912, RG59, IAG, box 3838, dispatch no. 284, pp. 1–3, NACP.

26. Cutter to Sands, 18 March 1910, RG59, IAG, box 3838, dispatch no. 100, pp. 1–2, NACP; Sands to Secretary of State, 2 April 1910, RG59, IAG, box 3838, NACP; Wilson to Secretary of State, 17 June 1912, RG59, IAG, box 3838, dispatch no. 284, pp. 1–3, NACP.

27. Cutter to Sands, 18 March 1910, RG59, IAG, box 3838, dispatch no. 100, pp. 1–2, NACP; Sands to Secretary of State, 2 April 1910, RG59, IAG, box 3838, NACP; Wilson to Secretary of State, 17 June 1912, RG59, IAG, box 3838, dispatch no. 284, pp. 1–3, NACP.

28. LaFeber, *Inevitable Revolutions*, 29–31; Gillick, "Life and Labor in a Banana Enclave," 13; Linebaugh and Rediker, *The Many-Headed Hydra*, 152.

29. Cutter to Sands, 10 January 1910, 25 February 1910, RG59, IAG, box 3838, NACP; Reed to Owen, 2 March 1910, RG84, vol. 140, NACP; Sands to Cutter, 9 March 1910, RG59, IAG, box 3838, NACP; British Consul Carden to Cutter, 15 March 1910, RG59, IAG, box 3838, NACP; Cutter to Sands, 18 March 1910, RG59, IAG, box 3838, dispatch no. 100, pp. 1–2, NACP.

30. Cutter to Sands, 10 January 1910, 25 February 1910, RG59, IAG, box 3838, NACP; Reed to Owen, 2 March 1910, RG84, vol. 140, NACP; Sands to Cutter, 9 March 1910, RG59, IAG, box 3838, NACP; British Consul Carden to Cutter, 15 March 1910, RG59, IAG, box 3838, NACP; Cutter to Sands, 18 March 1910, RG59, IAG, box 3838, dispatch no. 100, pp. 1–2, NACP.

31. Carden to Cutter, 15 March 1910, RG59, IAG, box 3838, dispatch no. 100, NACP; Cutter to Sands, 18 March 1910, RG59, IAG, box 3838, dispatch no. 100, pp. 1–2, NACP.

32. Carden to Cutter, 15 March 1910, RG59, IAG, box 3838, dispatch no. 100, NACP; Cutter to Sands, 18 March 1910, RG59, IAG, box 3838, dispatch no. 100, pp. 1–2, NACP; Cutter to Sands, 24 March 1910, RG59, IAG, box 3838, dispatch no. 100, p. 1, NACP.

33. Carden to Cutter, 15 March 1910, RG59, IAG, box 3838, dispatch no. 100, NACP; Cutter to Sands, 18 March 1910, RG59, IAG, box 3838, dispatch no. 100, pp. 1–2, NACP; Cutter to Sands, 24 March 1910, RG59, IAG, box 3838, dispatch no. 100, p. 1, NACP.

34. Carden to Cutter, 15 March 1910, RG59, IAG, box 3838, dispatch no. 100, NACP; Cutter to Sands, 18 March 1910, RG59, IAG, box 3838, dispatch no. 100, pp. 1–2, NACP; Cutter to Sands, 24 March 1910, RG59, IAG, box 3838, dispatch no. 100, p. 1, NACP; Reed to Sands, 25 August 1910, dispatch no. 199, NACP; unidentified author, 16 July 1910, MRE, leg. 6281, pp. 1–2, AGCA.

35. Carden to Cutter, 15 March 1910, RG59, IAG, box 3838, dispatch no. 100, NACP; Cutter to Sands, 18 March 1910, RG59, IAG, box 3838, dispatch no. 100, pp. 1–2, NACP; Cutter to Sands, 24 March 1910, RG59, IAG, box 3838, dispatch no. 100,

p. 1, NACP; Reed to Sands, 25 August 1910, dispatch no. 199, NACP; unidentified author, 16 July 1910, MRE, leg. 6281, pp. 1–2, AGCA.

36. Wilson to Secretary of State, 13 August 1913, RG59, IAG, box 3838, pp. 1–2, NACP; Victor M. Cutter to Luis Estrada Monzon, 16 August 1913, JPI, p. 2, AGCA.

37. Crafter to Superintendente de International Railroad of Central America, 3 April 1913, MF, International Railroad of Central America, "Telegramas cerca huelga" de 1913, leg. 15868, p. 3, AGCA.

38. Crafter to Superintendente de International Railroad of Central America, 3 April 1913, MF, International Railroad of Central America, "Telegramas cerca huelga" de 1913, leg. 15868, p. 3, AGCA.

39. *Diario de Centroamérica*, 4 April 1913, p. 1.

40. *Diario de Centroamérica*, 5 April 1913, p. 7.

41. Ibid.; F. G. Williamson to Ministro de Fomento, 15 April 1913, MF, leg. 15868, AGCA.

42. *Diario de Centroamérica*, 4 April 1913, 11 April 1913.

43. *Diario de Centroamérica*, 16 April 1913.

44. Legation of the United States of America to Ministerio de Relaciónes Exteriores, 22 April 1913, MRE, leg. 7597, Memorandum no. 382, AGCA.

45. Joaquin Hecht to Lipton, 23 January 1915, RG84, vol. 184, pp. 1–2, NACP; Lipton to Hecht, 26 January 1915, RG84, vol. 184, NACP.

46. Joaquin Hecht to Lipton, 23 January 1915, RG84, vol. 184, pp. 1–2, NACP.

47. Ibid.

48. Ibid.; Hecht to Lipton, 29 January 1915, RG84, vol. 184, pp. 1–2, NACP.

49. Hecht to Lipton, 29 January 1915, RG84, vol. 184, pp. 1–2, NACP.

50. Hecht to Lipton, 23 January 1915, RG84, vol. 184, pp. 1–2, NACP; Lipton to Hecht, 26 January 1915, RG84, vol. 184, pp. 1–2, NACP.

51. Cutter to Monzon, 16 August 1913, JPI, 1913, p. 2, AGCA.

52. Ibid.

53. Juzgado Municipal de Puerto Barrios to Jefatura Politica de Izabal, September 1913, JPI, 1913, AGCA.

54. *British Documents on Foreign Affairs—Reports and Papers from the Foreign Office Confidential Print*, 8:215.

55. Edward Reed to Jack Armstrong, 4 December 1918, Foreign Office 252, 543/ no. 119, United Kingdom Public Records Office.

56. Edward Reed to Jack Armstrong, 4 December 1918, Foreign Office 252, 543/ no. 119, United Kingdom Public Records Office.

57. Thurston to Secretary of State, 4 December 1918, 7 December 1918, 12 December 1918, RG59, roll 3, NACP; Thurston to Secretary of State, 30 January 1919, 17 February 1919, RG59, roll 20, NACP; Thurston to Secretary of State, 28 February 1919, roll 3, NACP.

Chapter 5. Labor Radicalism on the Caribbean Coast

1. Referring to the interpretation given in Asociación de Investigación y Estudios Sociales Dirección, *Más de 100 años del movimiento obrero urbano en guatemala*, 81–83; and García, "El movimimiento obrero en Guatemala, 1900–1954," 29–31.

2. Jefe Político de Izabal to Ministerio de Fomento, 10 February 1921, MF, leg. 15873, AGCA.

3. Walterman to Secretary of State, 31 January 1920, RG59, roll 3, dispatch no. 173, pp. 1–5, NACP.

4. Asociación de Investigación y Estudios Sociales Dirección, *Más de 100 años del movimiento obrero urbano en guatemala*, 74–77, 81–84; and García, "El movimimiento obrero en Guatemala, 1900–1954," 29–31.

5. McMillin to Secretary of State, 15 January 1920, 17 January 1920, 30 January 1920, RG59, roll 3, p. 586, NACP.

6. McMillin to Secretary of State, 15 January 1920, 17 January 1920, 30 January 1920, RG59, roll 3, p. 586, NACP; Walterman to Secretary of State, 31 January 1920, RG59, dispatch no. 173, pp. 1–5, NACP.

7. Jones, *Guatemala Past and Present*, 67; García, "El movimiento obrero en Guatemala, 1900–1954," 29–31; Asociación de Investigación y Estudios Sociales Dirección, *Más de 100 años del movimiento obrero urbano en guatemala*, 74, 88.

8. Liberal Club of Puerto Barrios to Comandante of the Port, 25 April 1915, JPI, 1915, paq. 3, AGCA.

9. Jefe Político de Izabal to Ministerio de Fomento, 10 February 1921, MF, leg. 15873, AGCA.

10. Gillick, "Life and Labor in a Banana Enclave," 202.

11. Ibid., 203.

12. Dosal, *Doing Business with the Dictators*, chap. 6; Asociación de Investigación y Estudios Sociales Dirección, Más de 100 años del movimiento obrero urbano en guatemala, 91, 105–6.

13. McMillin, 31 January 1920, RG59, roll 3, dispatch no. 173, pp. 1–5, NACP.

14. Ibid.

15. Ibid.

16. Ibid.

17. Asociación de Investigación y Estudios Sociales Dirección, *Más de 100 años del movimiento obrero urbano en guatemala*, 103.

18. García, "El movimiento obrero en Guatemala, 1900–1954," 44.

19. del Valle Pérez, "'El Partido Unionista' de Guatemala," 72, 76. Asociación de Investigación y Estudios Sociales Dirección, *Más de 100 años del movimiento obrero urbano en guatemala*, chap. 3, deals with the Ubico administration and labor organizations. Also see Sagastume, "La empresa de los ferrocarriles de Guatemala," 8–9; Grieb, *Guatemalan Caudillo*, 38–39, 42–44.

20. García, "El movimiento obrero en Guatemala, 1900–1954," 44.

21. Ibid.

22. Ibid., 49.

23. Dosal, *Doing Business with the Dictators*, 115–17, 119.

24. *Diario de Centroamérica*, 25 May 1920, p. 1, and 26 May 1920, p. 1.

25. Ibid.

26. *La Patria*, 4 June 1920.

27. Ibid.; *La Patria*, 7 June 1920.

28. McMillin to Secretary of State, 7 June 1920, RG59, roll 20, 353, USNA.

29. *La Patria*, 8 June 1920.

30. Ibid.

31. Minor C. Keith to Felix Castellanos B., 28 October 1920, MF, International Railroad of Central America, leg. 15870, p. 3, AGCA.

32. For more on Canal Zone labor history and race, see Conniff, *Black Labor on a White Canal*.

33. Herbert S. Gold to Luis P. Aguirre, 2 December 1920, MRE, leg. 8535, AGCA.

34. Forster, "Reforging National Revolution," 206–7.

35. Kepner, *Social Aspects of the Banana Industry*, 180–81, 184, 197.

36. Letwin, *The Challenge of Interracial Unionism*, 184.

37. Harpelle, *The West Indians of Costa Rica*, 50; Conniff, *Black Labor on a White Canal*, 26, 54–55, 59–60; Arnesen, *Waterfront Workers of New Orleans*, 230–36, 253.

38. Rosenthal, "Controlling the Line," 58; Dosal, *Doing Business with the Dictators*, chap. 7.

39. Asociación de Investigación y Estudios Sociales Dirección, *Más de 100 años del movimiento obrero urbano en guatemala*, 332–33; Dosal, *Doing Business with the Dictators*, 129.

40. Asociación de Investigación y Estudios Sociales Dirección, *Más de 100 años del movimiento obrero urbano en guatemala*, 332; Obando Sanchez, "Apuntes para la historia movimiento obrero de Guatemala," 77.

41. Dosal, *Doing Business with the Dictators*, 129; García, "El movimimiento obrero en Guatemala, 1900–1954," 46–47, 49.

42. Dosal, *Doing Business with the Dictators*, 129.

43. Burquist, *Labor and Latin America*, 11.

44. Brown, "The Panama Canal," 472, 474–75.

45. Chomsky, *Indian Workers and the United Fruit Company in Costa Rica*, 209–10, 215, 221; Harpelle, *The West Indians of Costa Rica*, 50.

46. Dosal, *Doing Business with the Dictators*, 120.

47. Jefe Político de Izabal to Ministerio de Fomento, 11 January 1921, JPI, 1921, paq. 1, no. 157, AGCA.

48. Jefe Político de Izabal to Castellano, 5 February 1921, JPI, 1921, paq. 1, no. 866, AGCA; transcription of a 27 January 1921 note, JPI, 1921, paq. 1, AGCA.

49. *La Patria*, 14 January 1921.

50. *La Patria*, 22 January 1921.

51. *La Patria*, 14 January 1921, p. 4; *La Patria*, 22 January 1921, p. 7.

52. Jefe Político de Izabal to Castellano, 10 February 1921, MF, leg. 15873, AGCA; *Diario de Centroamérica*, April 26, 1921.

53. Transcribed letter of Castellano (dated 11 February 1921), 12 February 1921, MF, leg. 15873, AGCA.

54. *El Unionista*, 26 April 1921.

55. *Diario de Centroamérica*, 26 April 1921.

56. Ibid.

57. "Solución de la huelga del Ferrocarril," ca. 26 April 1921, pp. 1–3, MF, leg. 1587, AGCA. The list contains the names of workers from various departments within the International Railroad of Central America, including wages scales; the list of names for the executive committee shows no North American surnames.

58. "Solución de la huelga del Ferrocarril," ca. 26 April 1921, pp. 1–3, MF, leg. 1587, AGCA.

59. *Diario de Centroamérica*, 26 April 1921; *Censo general de la población de la República de Guatemala . . . 1921.*

60. *Diario de Centroamérica*, 26 April 1921; *Censo general de la población de la República de Guatemala . . . 1921.*

61. *Diario de Centroamérica*, 26 April 1921.

62. *Excelsior*, 9 March 1922.

63. *Excelsior*, 2 March 1922.

64. *Excelsior*, 15 May 1922.

65. *Excelsior*, 21 September 1922.

66. Transcribed Telegrams, 5 February 1923, MF, Despacho de Fomento Ano de 1923, leg. 22091, exp. 3361, Compania Frutera, AGCA.

67. Ibid.

68. Geissler to Secretary of State, 10 February 1923, RG59, roll 20, p. 354, NACP.

69. Frost to Secretary of State, 7 February 1923, RG59, roll 20, pp. 355–36, NACP.

70. Ferguson telegram, reprinted in *El Imparcial*, 21 February 1923.

71. Thomas, 3–19 February 1923, RG59, roll 20, pp. 368–73, NACP.

72. Ibid.

73. Ibid.

74. Ibid.

75. Ibid.

76. Ibid.

77. Thomas to Ministro de Fomento, 3 February 1923, MF, Despacho de Fomento, Ano de 1923, Transcribed Telegrams, leg. 22091, exp. 3361, Compania Frutera, AGCA.

78. Thomas to Ministro de Fomento, 3 February 1923, MF, Despacho de Fomento, Ano de 1923, Transcribed Telegrams, leg. 22091, exp. 3361, Compania Frutera, AGCA; Julio Molina to Presidente de la República de Guatemala, 6 February 1923, Puerto Barrios, MF, leg. 2209, exp. 3361, AGCA.

79. Thomas to Ministro de Fomento, 3 February 1923, MF, Despacho de Fomento, Ano de 1923, Transcribed Telegrams, leg. 22091, exp. 3361, Compania Frutera, AGCA; Julio Molina to Presidente de la República de Guatemala, 6 February 1923, Puerto Barrios, MF, leg. 2209, exp. 3361, AGCA.

80. *El Imparcial*, 17 February 1923, p. 6.

81. *El Imparcial*, 27 February 1923.

82. *El Imparcial*, 19 February 1923.

83. *El Imparcial*, 19 February 1923.

84. Ibid.

85. Ibid.

86. Geissler to Secretary of State, 15 February 1923, RG59, roll 20, pp. 360–61, NACP.

87. *El Imparcial*, 15 February 1923, 16 February 1923; Thomas, 24 February 1923, RG59, roll 20 382–86, NACP.

88. Telegram, reprinted in *El Imparcial*, 21 February 1923.

89. Ibid.; Geissler to Secretary of State, 3 March 1923, RG59, roll 20, dispatch no. 199, pp. 362–64, NACP.

90. *El Imparcial*, 6 March 1923

91. Dosal, *Doing Business with the Dictators*, 133.

92. *El Imparcial*, 6 March 1923.

93. Thomas, 3–19 February 1923, RG59, roll 20, pp. 373–76, NACP.

94. Ibid.

95. Geissler to Secretary of State, 10 March 1923, RG59, roll 20, dispatch no. 199, pp. 365–66, NACP.

96. Dosal, *Doing Business with the Dictators*, 134.

97. *El Imparcial*, 15 February 1923, 6 March 1923.

98. Ibid.

99. Ibid.

100. Ibid.

101. Herbert S. Gold to Luis P. Aguirre, 2 December 1920, MRE, leg. 8535, AGCA.

102. García, "El movimimiento obrero en Guatemala, 1900–1954," 48.

Chapter 6. We Depend on Others Too Much

1. Martin, *Marcus Garvey, Hero*, 54; A. Percy Bennett to Earl Curzon, 7 April 1921, "Panamá, Report for the Period, 1914–1920," received 9 May 1921, document 181-182,

enclosure in document 181, in *British Documents on Foreign Affairs—Reports and Papers from the Foreign Office Confidential Print*, 8:215–17.

2. Mulzac, *A Star to Steer*, 74–77.

3. Martin, *Race First*, 16.

4. Mulzac, *A Star to Steer*, 76.

5. Marcus Garvey, Panama speech given on 3 May 1921, reproduced in the *Negro World*, 4 June 1921, p. 5.

6. Ibid.

7. Ibid.

8. Mulzac, *A Star to Steer*, 76.

9. Ibid., 189.

10. Edward Reed to the Galveston Chamber of Commerce, 11 May 1908, RG84, vol. 13, NACP; Edward Reed to Brown Shoe Company, 22 June 1917, RG84, vol. 28, NACP; Penney Diary, 112–13, 134, 141; Williams, "The Rise of the Banana Industry," 117–18.

11. *Negro World*, 19 March 1921, pp. 8–9; 26 March 1921, p. 6; 23 April 1921, p. 9.

12. Martin, *Race First*, 15–16, 69–70; Martin, *Marcus Garvey, Hero*, 82–83; Harpelle, *The West Indians of Costa Rica*, 53.

13. Martin, *Race First*, 17, 189.

14. For descriptions of the activities of the Latin American branches, see *Negro World*, 19 February 1921; 19 March 1921; and 26 March 1921.

15. Linebaugh and Rediker, *The Many-Headed Hydra*, 61, 77; Kelley, "We Are Not What We Seem," 197.

16. Stein, *The World of Marcus Garvey*, 143.

17. *Negro World*, 26 March 1921, p. 10.

18. *Negro World*, 19 March 1921, p. 4.

19. Cronon, *Black Moses*, 195–96, 222; Martin, *Marcus Garvey, Hero*, 55–56; Martin, *Race First*, 31, 182; Stein, *The World of Marcus Garvey*, 143.

20. Martin, *Race First*, 31.

21. Ibid.

22. James, *Holding Aloft the Banner of Ethiopia*, 51, 64–66; Martin, *Marcus Garvey, Hero*, 59, 77–78; Martin, *The Pan-African Connection*, 54–56.

23. Williams, "The Rise of the Banana Industry," 118–19.

24. "Guatemala Gets on the Map: U. N. I.A. Branch, with C. S. Bourne as Local Leader, Holds Enthusiastic Meeting—One Man Buys 200 Shares," *Negro World*, New York, 28 August 1920.

25. Hill, *The Marcus Garvey and Universal Negro Improvement Association Papers*, 2:514–15.

26. Ibid.

27. Martin, *Marcus Garvey, Hero*, 60, 63.

28. Hill, *The Marcus Garvey and Universal Negro Improvement Association Papers*, 2:514–15.

29. "Marcus Garvey and Miss H. V. Davis Tell Thrilling Story of Trip to West Indies and Central America," *Negro World*, 30 July 1921, p. 3.

30. Martin, *Marcus Garvey*, 49; Martin, *Race First*, 236–37.

31. "Second International Convention of Negroes," *Negro World*, 3 September 1921.

32. Beals, *Banana Gold*, 148–52.

Epilogue

1. Garrard Harris, 1914, RG84, vol. 179, NACP.

2. Handy, *Gift of the Devil*, 27–28.

3. Ibid., 27–29.

4. Mary Anastasia O'Grady, "Americas: Train Wreck in Guatemala," *Wall Street Journal*, 23 July 2007, p. A14.

5. Levenson-Estrada, *Trade Unionists against Terror*.

Bibliography

Archival Sources

Archivo General de Centro América. Guatemala City, Guatemala.
  Jefatura Política (records for Departments of Retalhuleu, Alta Verapaz, and Izabal), 1896–1925
  Ministerio de Fomento, Signatura B, Legajos, 1884–1928
  Ministerio de Relaciónes Exteriores, Signatura B, Legajos, 1884–1928
  Ministerio de Gobernación y Justicia, Signatura B, Legajos, 1884–1928
Collección de Venezuela. Hemeroteca Naciónal de la Biblioteca Naciónal de Guatemala. Guatemala City, Guatemala.
National Archives at College Park. College Park, Md.
  General Records of the Department of State (Record Group 59)
  Records of the Foreign Service Posts of the Department of State (Record Group 84)
  Records of the Office of the Comptroller of the Currency (Record Group 101)
National Archives Building. Washington, D.C.
  Records of the Bureau of Naval Personnel (Record Group 24)
Penney, William T., Manuscript. Latin American Library, Tulane University, Rare Book and Manuscript Department. New Orleans.
Tunnell Family, Letters, 1894-95. Cornell University Library, Special Collections. Ithaca, N.Y.

Published Sources

Acuña Ortega, Victor Hugo, ed. *Historia general de Centro América*. Vol. 4, *Las repúblicas agroexportadoras (1870–1945)*. Costa Rica: Facultad Latinoamericana de Ciencias Sociales, Programa Costa Rica, 1994.
Adams, Frederick. *Conquest of the Tropics: Story of the Creative Enterprises Conducted by the United Fruit Company*. New York: Doubleday, Page & Co., 1914.
Adams, Richard N. *Encuesta sobre la cultura de los ladinos en Guatemala*. Guatemala: Editorial del Ministerio de Educación Pública, 1956.
Aguilar Bulgarelli, Oscar. *La huelga de los tútiles, 1887–1889: Un capítulo de nuestra historia social*. San José, Costa Rica: Editorial Universidad Estatal a Distancia, 1989.
Andrews, George Reid. "Review Essay: Latin American Workers." *Journal of Social History* 21 (Winter 1987): 311–26.

Aptheker, Herbert, ed. *A Documentary History of the Negro People of the United States*. Vol. 1, *From Colonial Times through the Civil War*. Preface by W.E.B. Du Bois. New York: The Citadel Press, 1951.

Armstrong, Louis. *Satchmo: My Life in New Orleans*. New York: Da Capo Press, 1986.

Arnesen, Eric. *Brotherhoods of Color: Black Railroad Workers and the Struggle for Equality*. Cambridge, Mass.: Harvard University Press, 2001.

———. "'Like Banquo's Ghost, It Will Not Down': The Race Question and the American Railroad Brotherhoods, 1880–1920." *American Historical Review* 99 (December 1994): 1601–33.

———. *Waterfront Workers of New Orleans: Race, Class, and Politics, 1863–1923*. Oxford: Oxford University Press, 1991.

Asociación de Investigación y Estudios Sociales Dirección. *Más de 100 años del movimiento obrero urbano en guatemala*. Vol. 1, *Artesanos y obreros en el periodo liberal (1877–1944)*. Guatemala: Editorial Piedra Santa, 1991.

Asturias, Miguel Angel. *El Papa Verde*. Translated by Gregory Rabassa. New York: Delacorte Press, 1971.

———. *Strong Wind*. Translated by Gregory Rabassa. New York: Delacorte Press, 1968.

Bak, Joan L. "Labor, Community, and the Making of a Cross-Class Alliance in Brazil: The 1917 Railroad Strikes in Rio Grande do Sul." *Hispanic American Historical Review* 78 (May 1998): 179–227.

Balcárcel, José Luis. "El movimiento obrero en Guatemala." In vol. 2 of *Historia del movimiento obrero en América Latina*, ed. Pablo Gonález Casanova. Mexico City: Siglo XXI, 1985.

Balderrama, Francisco E., and Raymond Rodríguez. *Decade of Betrayal: Mexican Repatriation in the 1930s*. Albuquerque: University of New Mexico Press, 1995.

Barahona, Marvin. *La hegemonía de los Estados Unidos en Honduras (1907–1932)*. Tegucigalpa, Honduras: Centro de Documentación de Honduras, 1989.

Batres, Alejandra. "The Experience of the Guatemalan United Fruit Company Workers, 1944–1954: Why Did They Fail?" (1995 LLILAS Distinguished Paper Award, University of Texas-Austin). Texas Papers on Latin America, no. 95-01, 1995.

Beals, Carleton. *Banana Gold*. Philadelphia: J. B. Lippincott, 1932.

Benjamin, Thomas, Timothy Hall, and David Rutherford. *The Atlantic World in the Age of Empire*. Boston: Houghton Mifflin, 2001.

Berlin, Ira, Marc Favreau, and Steven F. Miller, eds. *Remembering Slavery: African Americans Talk about Their Personal Experiences of Slavery*. New York: The New Press; Washington, D.C.: In association with the Library of Congress, 1998.

Bethel, Leslie, ed. *The Independence of Latin America*. Cambridge: Cambridge University Press, 1987.

Blassingame, John W. *Black New Orleans, 1860–1880*. Chicago: University of Chicago Press, 1973.

Blumer-Thomas, Victor. *The Economic History of Latin America since Independence.* Cambridge: Cambridge University Press, 1994.

Bonnet, Aubrey W., and Llewelyn G. Watson, eds. *Emerging Perspectives on the Black Diaspora.* Lanham, Md.: University Press of America, 1990.

Bourgois, Phillipe I. *Ethnicity at Work: Divided Labor on a Central American Banana Plantation.* Baltimore: Johns Hopkins University Press, 1989.

Bracey, John H., Jr., August Meier, and Elliott Rudwick, eds. *Black Workers and Organized Labor.* Belmont, Calif.: Wadsworth Publishers, 1971.

Braudel, Fernand. *Civilization and Capitalism, 15th–18th Century.* Translation from the French revised by Siân Reynolds. 3 vols. New York, 1982–1984. (Original French edition, 1979)

Brigham, William T. *Guatemala: The Land of the Quetzal.* New York: Charles Scribner's Sons, 1887.

British Documents on Foreign Affairs—Reports and Papers from the Foreign Office Confidential Print. Part I, From the Mid-Nineteenth Century to the First World War. Series D, Latin America, 1845–1914. Vols. 7–8, *Central America, 1856–1886* and 1887–1914. General editors, Kenneth Bourne and D. Cameron Watt; volume editor, George Philip. Bethesda, Md.: University Publications of America, 1991.

Brock, Lisa, and Digna Castañeda Fuertes. *Between Race and Empire: African-Americans and Cubans before the Cuban Revolution.* Philadelphia: Temple University Press, 1998.

Brown, Jonathan C. "Foreign and Native-Born Workers in Porfirian, Mexico." *American Historical Review* 98 (June 1993): 786–818.

Brown, Patrice C. "The Panama Canal: The African American Experience." In "Federal Records and African American History," ed. John W. Carlin. Special Issue, *Prologue* 29 (Summer 1997). Online at http://www.archives.gov/publications/prologue/1997/summer/panama-canal.html.

Bulmer-Thomas, Victor. *The Economic History of Latin America since Independence.* Cambridge: Cambridge University Press, 1994.

———. *The Political Economy of Central America since 1920.* Cambridge: Cambridge University Press, 1987.

Burbank, Addison. *Guatemala Profile.* New York: Coward-McCann, 1939.

Burgquist, Charles. *Labor and Latin America: Comparative Essays on Chile, Argentina, Venezuela, and Columbia.* Stanford, Calif.: Stanford University Press, 1986.

Burns, E. Bradford. *The Poverty of Progress: Latin America in the Nineteenth Century.* Berkeley: University of California Press, 1980.

Cambranes, J. C., ed. *500 años de lucha por la tierra: Estudios sobre propiedad rural y reforma agraria en Guatemala.* 2 vols. Guatemala: FLACSO, 1992.

Carpenter, Frank G. *Lands of the Caribbean.* New York: Double Day, Page & Co., 1926.

Carrillo Ramírez, Salomón. *Tierras de oriente.* Guatemala City, 1927.

Casanova, Pablo Gonález, ed. *Historia del movimiento obrero en América Latina,* vol. 2. Mexico City: Siglo XXI, 1985.

Chang, Ching Chieh. "The Chinese in Latin America: A Preliminary Geographical Survey with Special Reference to Cuba and Jamaica." Ph.D. diss., University of Maryland, 1956.

Chang Sagastume, German. *Monografía del Departamento de Izabal: Un estudio detallado de la historia y geografía que todos deben conocer*. Guatemala City, 1989.

Chapman, Peter. *Jungle Capitalists: A Story of Globalisation, Greed, and Revolution*. Edinburgh: Cannongate, 2007.

Chomsky, Aviva. *West Indian Workers and the United Fruit Company in Costa Rica, 1870–1940*. Baton Rouge: Louisiana State University Press, 1996.

Chomsky, Aviva, and Aldo Lauria-Santiago, eds. *Identity and Struggle at the Margins of the Nation State: The Laboring Peoples of Central America and the Hispanic Caribbean*. Durham, N.C.: Duke University Press, 1998.

Clarke, John Henrik, ed., with Amy Jaques Garvey. *Marcus Garvey and the African Vision*. New York: Random House, 1974.

Clifford, James. "Diaspora." *Cultural Anthropology* 9, no. 3 (August 1994): 302–38.

Cohen, William. "Negro Involuntary Servitude in the South, 1865–1940: A Preliminary Analysis." *Journal of Southern History* 42 (February 1976): 30–60.

Conniff, Michael. *Black Labor on a White Canal: Panama, 1904–1981*. Pittsburgh: University of Pittsburgh Press, 1985.

Cooper, Frederick, Allen Isaacman, Florencia E. Mallon, William Roseberry, and Steven J. Stern, eds. *Confronting Historical Paradigms: Peasants, Labor, and the Capitalist World System in Africa and Latin America*. Madison: University of Wisconsin Press, 1993.

Cox, Oliver Cromwell. *Caste, Class, & Race: A Study in Social Dynamics*. Garden City, N.Y.: Doubleday, 1948.

Crisanto Meléndez, Armando, and Uayujuru Savaranga. *Adeija sisira gererun aguburigu garinagu: "El enojo de las sonajas: Palabras del ancestro."* Tegucigalpa, Honduras: Graficentro Eidtores, 1997.

Cronon, E. David. *Black Moses: The Story of Marcus Garvey and the United Negro Improvement Association*. Madison: University of Wisconsin Press, 1969.

Crowther, Samuel. *The Romance and Rise of the American Tropics*. Garden City, NY: Doubleday, Doran & Co., 1929.

Cunningham, Eugene. *Gypsying through Central America*. Photographs by Norman Hartman. New York: E. P. Dutton, 1922.

Dailey, Jane. *Before Jim Crow: The Politics of Race in Postemancipation Virginia*. Chapel Hill: University of North Carolina Press, 2000.

Dailey, Jane, Glenda Elizabeth Gilmore, and Bryant Simon, eds. *Jumpin' Jim Crow: Southern Politics from Civil War to Civil Rights*. Princeton, N.J.: Princeton University Press, 2000.

Dann, Martin E., ed. *The Black Press, 1827–1890: The Quest of National Identity*. New York: G. P. Putnams' Sons, 1971.

Davis, Richard Harding. *Three Gringos in Venezuela and Central America*. New York: Harper & Brothers, 1896.

de León Aragón, Oscar. *Los contratos de la United Fruit Company y las compañias muellaras en Guatemala: Estudio histórico-jurídico*. Guatemala: Editorial del Ministerio de Educación Pública, 1950.

del Valle Pérez, Hernán. "'El Partido Unionista' de Guatemala, su participation en el derrocamiento de Manuel Estrada Cabrera, y en el gobierno de Carlos Herrera, 1919–1921." Tesis Licenciatura en Historia, Universidad de San Carlos de Guatemala Escuela de Historia, 1975.

de Villeda Mainieri, Amparo García. "Algunos aspectos de la economía de Guatemala de 1892 a 1898." *Estudios: Instituto de Investigaciones Historicas, Antropologicas y Arquelogicas* (Guatemala) 8. (March 1981): 9–104.

Diacon, Todd A. *Millenarian Vision, Capitalist Reality: Brazil's Contestado Rebellion, 1912–1916*. Durham, N.C.: Duke University Press, 1991.

Domínguez, Jorge I., ed. *Race and Ethnicity in Latin America*. New York: Garland Publishing, 1994.

Dosal, Paul J. *Doing Business with the Dictators: A Political History of United Fruit in Guatemala, 1899–1944*. Wilmington, Del.: Scholarly Resources, 1993.

———. *Industrial Oligarchies: The Rise of Guatemala's Ruling Elite, 1871–1994*. Westport, Conn.: Praeger, 1995.

Drimmer, Melvin, ed. *Black History: A Reappraisal*. Garden City, N.Y.: Doubleday, 1968.

Du Bois, W. E. B. *The Souls of Black Folk*. 3rd ed. New York: Dover Publications, 1994.

Dunkerley, James. *Power in the Isthmus: A Political History of Modern Central America*. London: Verso, 1988.

Echeverri-Gent, Elisavinda. "Forgotten Workers: British West Indians and the Early Days of the Banana Industry in Costa Rica and Honduras." *Journal of Latin American Studies* 24 (May 1992): 275–308.

Elliot, L. E. *Central America: New Paths in Ancient Lands*. New York: Dodd, Mead and Co., 1925.

Engerman, Stanley L., Manuel Moreno Fraginals, and Frank Moya Pons, eds. *Between Slavery and Free Labor: The Spanish-Speaking Caribbean in the Nineteenth Century*. Baltimore: Johns Hopkins University Press, 1985.

Euraque, Darío A. *Reinterpreting the Banana Republic: Region and State in Honduras, 1870–1972*. Chapel Hill: University of North Carolina Press, 1996.

Fax, Elton C. *Garvey: The Story of a Pioneer Black Nationalist*. New York: Dodd, Mead & Co., 1972.

Fernández, Juan Jose. *Las huelgas*. San Salvador: El Salvador, 1920.

Foner, Eric. *Reconstruction: America's Unfinished Revolution, 1863–1877*. New York: HarperCollins, 1988.

Foner, Philip S. *Organized Labor and the Black Worker, 1619–1973*. New York: Praeger, 1974.

Forster, Cindy. "Reforging National Revolution: Campesino Labor Struggles in Guatemala, 1944–1956." In *Identity and Struggle at the Margins of the Nation State: The Laboring Peoples of Central America and the Hispanic Caribbean*, edited bt Aviva Chomsky and Aldo Lauria-Santiago. Durham, N.C.: Duke University Press, 1998.

Fraginals, Manuel Moreno, Frank Moya Pons, and Stanely L. Engerman, eds. *Between Slavery and Free Labor: The Spanish-Speaking Caribbean in the Nineteenth Century*. Baltimore: Johns Hopkins University Press, 1985.

French, John D. *The Brazilian Workers' ABC*. Chapel Hill: University of North Carolina Press, 1992.

Gage, Thomas. *A New Survey of the West Indies, 1648: The English-American*. Edited with an introduction by A. P. Newton. New York: Robert M. McBride, 1929.

García, Jose Barnoya. *Los cien años del insecto*. 2nd ed. Guatemala City: Modernas, 1996.

García, María Elena Recinos. "El movimimiento obrero en Guatemala, 1900–1954." Tesis Licenciatura en Historia, Universidad de San Carlos de Guatemala Escuela de Historia, 1977.

García Márquez, Gabriel. *One Hundred Years of Solitude*. New York: Harper & Row, 1970.

Gargallo, Francesca, and Adalberto Santana. *Belice: Sus fronteras y destino*. Mexico City: Universidad Nacional Autónoma de México, 1993.

Garrido Toriello, Guillermo. *Tras la cortina de banano*. Mexico City: Fondo de Cultura Economica, 1976.

Gaspar, Jeffrey Casey. *Limón, 1880–1940: Un estudio de la industria bananera en Costa Rica*. San Jose: Editorial Costa Rica, 1979.

Gillick, Steven S. "Life and Labor in a Banana Enclave: Bananeros, the United Fruit Company and the Limits of Trade Unionism in Guatemala, 1906–1931." Ph.D. diss., Tulane University, 1995.

Gilroy, Paul. *The Black Atlantic: Double Consciousness, and Modernity*. Cambridge: Harvard University Press, 1993.

González Davison, Fernando. *El régimen liberal en Guatemala (1871–1944)*. Guatemala: Editorial Universitaria, Universidad de San Carlos De Guatemala, 1987.

González, Nancie L. Solien. *Black Carib Household Structure: A Study of Migration and Modernization*. Seattle: University of Washington Press, 1969.

Gordon, Edmund T. *Disparate Diasporas: Identity and Politics in an African Nicaraguan Community*. Austin: University of Texas Press, 1998.

Graham, Richard. *The Idea of Race in Latin America, 1870–1940*. Austin: University of Texas Press, 1990.

Green, Lorenzo Johnston, and Carter G. Woodson. *The Negro Wage Earner*. New York: Russell & Russell, 1930.

Grieb, Kenneth J., ed. *Guatemalan Caudillo, The Regime of Jorge Ubico: Guatemala, 1931–1944*. Athens: Ohio University Press, 1979.

———. *Research Guide to Central America and the Caribbean.* Madison: University of Wisconsin Press, 1985.

Griffith, William J. *Empires in the Wilderness: Foreign Colonization and Development in Guatemala, 1834–1844.* Chapel Hill: University of North Carolina Press, 1965.

———. "The Historiography of Central America since 1830." *Hispanic American Historical Review* 40 (November 1960): 548–69.

Grossberg, Lawrence, ed. *Cultural Studies.* New York: Routledge Press, 1992.

Guatemala. Direccio´n General de Estadi´stica. *Censo general de la República de Guatemala levantado en 26 de febrero de 1893 por la Direccio´n General de estadi´stica y con los auspicios del presidente constitucional, General Don Jose´ Mari´a Reina Barrios.* Guatemala: Tipografía y Encuadernación "Nacional," 1894.

———. *Censo general de la población de la República de Guatemala levantado el 28 de agosto de 1921.* 2 vols. Guatemala: Tipografia Nacional, 1924.

Gudmundson, Lowell, and Héctor Lindo-Fuentes. *Central America, 1821–1871: Liberalism before Liberal Reform.* Tuscaloosa: University of Alabama Press, 1995.

Guerra-Borges, Alfredo. "Comunicaciones internas y puertos." In *Desde la República Federal hasta 1898,* vol. 4 of *Historia general de Guatemala.* Guatemala City: Asociación de Amigos del País Fundación para la Cultura y el Desarrollo, 1995.

Gutman, Herbert G. *The Black Family in Slavery and Freedom, 1750–1925.* New York: Vintage Books, 1976.

Hall, Linda B. *Álvaro Obregón: Power and Revolution in Mexico, 1911–1920.* College Station: Texas A&M University Press, 1981.

Handy, Jim. *Gift of the Devil: A History of Guatemala.* Boston: South End Press, 1984.

Harpelle, Ronald N. *The West Indians of Costa Rica: Race, Class, and the Integration of an Ethnic Minority.* Montreal: McGill–Queen's University Press, 2001.

Harris, William H. *The Harder We Run: Black Workers since the Civil War.* New York: Oxford University Press, 1982.

Haskin, Frederick J. *The Panama Canal.* New York: Doubleday, Page & Co., 1914.

Helg, Aline. *Our Rightful Share: The Afro-Cuban Struggle for Equality, 1886–1912.* Chapel Hill: University of North Carolina Press, 1995.

Herrera, Robinson. "The African Slave Trade in Early Santiago." *Urban History Workshop Review* 4 (Fall 1998): 6–12.

Hesse-Wartegy, Ernst von. *Travels on the Lower Mississippi, 1879–1880: A Memoir.* Edited and translated by Frederic Trautman. Columbia: University of Missouri Press, 1990.

Hill, Robert A., ed. *The Marcus Garvey and Universal Negro Improvement Association Papers.* Vol. 2, 27 August 1919–31 August 1920. Berkeley: University of California Press, 1983.

Historia general de Guatemala. Vol. 4, *Desde la República Federal hasta 1898.* Guatemala City: Asociación de Amigos del País Fundación para la Cultura y el Desarrollo, 1995.

Holloway, Thomas H. *Immigrants on the Land: Coffee and Society in São Paulo, 1886–1934.* Chapel Hill: University of North Carolina Press, 1980.

Informe ferrocarril al Norte Ministro de Fomento. Guatemala City: Tipografía Nacional, 1895.

Irwin, Graham W., ed. *Africans Abroad: A Documentary History of the Black Diaspora in Asia, Latin America, and the Caribbean during the Age of Slavery.* New York: Columbia University Press, 1977.

Jackson, Joy J. *New Orleans in the Gilded Age: Politics and Urban Progress, 1880–1896.* Louisiana: Louisiana State University Press, 1969.

James, Winston. *Holding Aloft the Banner of Ethiopia: Caribbean Radicalism in Early Twentieth-Century America.* London: Verso, 1998.

Jimenez Rivera, Dario Medardo. "El golpe de estado del 6 de diciembre de 1921 al gobierno de Carlos Herrera Luna." Tesis Licenciatura en Historia, Universidad de San Carlos de Guatemala Escuela de Historia, 1996.

Jones, Chester Lloyd. *Guatemala Past and Present.* Minneapolis: University of Minnesota Press, 1940.

Jones, J. Bascom, William T. Scoullar, and Máximo Soto Hall, eds. *El "Libro azul" de Guatemala, 1915.* New Orleans: Impreso por Searcy & Pfaff, 1915.

Joseph, G. M. *Revolution from Without: Yucatán, Mexico, and the United States, 1880–1924.* New York: Cambridge University Press, 1982.

Kaimowitz, David. "New Perspectives on Central American History, 1838–1945." *Latin American Research Review* 31 (1996): 201–10.

Karnes, Thomas L. *Tropical Enterprise: Standard Fruit and Steamship Company in Latin America.* Baton Rouge: Louisiana State University Press, 1978.

Kelley, Robin D. G., "'But a Local Phase of a World Problem': Black History's Global Vision, 1883–1950." *Journal of American History* 86 (December 1999): 1045–77.

Kelly, Brian. *Race, Class, and Power in the Alabama Coalfields, 1908–1921.* Urbana: University of Illinois Press, 2001.

Kelly, Robin D. G. "'But a Local Phase of a World Problem': Black History's Global Vision, 1883–1950." *Journal of American History* 86 (December 1999): 1055–58.

———. *Race Rebels: Culture, Politics, and the Black Working Class.* New York: The Free Press, 1996.

Kepner, Charles David, Jr. *Social Aspects of the Banana Industry.* New York: Columbia University Press, 1936.

Kepner, Charles David, Jr., and Jay Henry Soothill. *The Banana Empire: A Case Study of Economic Imperialism.* 1935; reprint, New York: Russell & Russell, 1963.

Knight, Franklin W., and Colin A. Palmer, eds. *The Modern Caribbean.* Chapel Hill: University of North Carolina Press, 1989.

Komisaruk, Catherine. "'The Work It Cost Me': The Struggles of Slaves and Free Africans in Guatemala, 1770–1825." *Urban History Workshop Review* 5 (Fall 1999): 4–24.

Kunst, J. "Notes on Negroes in Guatemala during the Seventeenth Century." *Journal of Negro History* 4 (October 1916): 390–97.

LaFeber, Walter. *Inevitable Revolutions: The United States in Central America.* New York: W. W. Norton, 1984.

Lemus, Jose Archila. *Monografía del Departamento de Zacapa.* Guatemala City: Tipografía Nacional, 1928.

Leonard, Thomas M., and Louis A. Peréz Jr. *A Guide to Central American Collections in the United States.* Reference Guides to Archival and Manuscripts Sources in World History, no. 3. Westport, Conn.: Greenwood Press, 1994.

Leopoldo, Zea. *The Latin American Mind.* Translated by James H. Abbott and Lowell Dunham. Norman: University of Oklahoma Press, 1963.

Letwin, Daniel. *The Challenge of Interracial Unionism: Alabama Coal Miners, 1878–1921.* Chapel Hill: University of North Carolina Press, 1998.

Levenson-Estrada, Deborah. *Trade Unionists against Terror: Guatemala City, 1954–1985.* Chapel Hill: University of North Carolina Press, 1994.

Lewis, Earl. *In Their Own Interests: Race, Class, and Power in Twentieth-Century Norfolk, Virginia.* Berkeley: University of California Press, 1991.

Lewis, Rupert, and Maureen Warner-Lewis, eds. *Garvey: Africa, Europe, the Americas.* Trenton, N.J.: African World Press, 1994.

Licht, Walter. *Working for the Railroad: The Organization of Work in the Nineteenth Century.* Princeton, N.J.: Princeton University Press, 1983.

Lichtenstein, Alex. *Twice the Work of Free Labor: The Political Economy of Convict Labor in the New South.* London: Verso, 1996.

Linebaugh, Peter, and Marcus Rediker. *The Many-Headed Hydra: Sailors, Slaves, Commoners, and the Hidden History of the Revolutionary Atlantic.* Boston: Beacon Press, 2000.

Litwack, Leon F. *Trouble in Mind: Black Southerners in the Age of Jim Crow.* New York: Alfred A. Knopf, 1998.

Lokken, Paul Thomas. "Afro-Indigenous Guatemala: The Pacific Coast in the Seventeenth Century." Paper presented at the 33rd annual New England Council on Latin American Studies (NECLAS) meeting, College of the Holy Cross, Worcester, Mass., October 2002.

———. "From Black to *Ladino*: People of African Descent, *Mestizaje*, and Racial Hierarchy in Rural Colonial Guatemala, 1600–1730." Ph.D. diss., University of Florida, 2000.

———. "A Maroon Moment: Rebel Slavery in Seventh-Century Guatemala." *Slavery & Abolition* 25 (December 2004): 44–58.

———. "Undoing Racial Hierarchy: Mulatos and Militia Service in Colonial Guatemala." *Journal of the Southern Council on Latin American Studies* 31 (November 1999): 25–36.

Louisiana Writer's Program. New York: Hastings House Publishers, 1940.

Lovell, John. *Stevedores and Dockers: A Study of Trade Unionism in the Port of London, 1870–1914.* New York: A. M. Kelley, 1960.

Lutz, Christopher H. *Santiago de Guatemala: City, Caste, and the Colonial Experience.* Norman: University of Oklahoma Press, 1994.

Lutz, Christopher, and Matthew Restall. "Wolves and Sheep? Black–Maya Relations in Colonial Guatemala and Yucatan." In *Beyond Black and Red: African–Native Relations in Colonial Latin America*, ed. Matthew Restall. Albuquerque: University of New Mexico Press, 2005.

Mack, Gerstle. *The Land Divided, A History of the Panama Canal and Other Isthmian Canal Projects.* New York: Knopf, 1944.

Marble, Manning. *How Capitalism Underdeveloped Black America: Problems in Race, Political Economy, and Society.* Boston: South End Press, 1980.

Martí, José. *Our America: Writings on Latin America and the Struggle for Cuban Independence.* Edited by Philip S. Foner. New York: Monthly Review Press, 1977.

———. *Obras completas.* 27 vols. Havana: Editorial Nacional de Cuba, 1963–1965.

Martín, Sagrera. *Los racismos en América "Latina": Sus colonialismos externos e internos.* Buenos Aires: Ediciones La Bastilla, 1974.

Martin, Tony. *Marcus Garvey, Hero: A First Biography.* Dover, Mass.: Majority Pres, 1983.

———. *Race First: The Ideological and Organizational Struggles of Marcus Garvey and the Universal Negro Improvement Association.* Dover, Mass.: Majority Press, 1986.

———. *The Pan-African Connection: From Slavery to Garvey and Beyond.* Dover, Mass.: Majority Pres, 1983.

Martínez Montiel, Luz María. *Negros en América.* Madrid: Editorial Mapfre, 1992.

McCreery, David J. "Coffee and Class: The Structure of Development in Liberal Guatemala." *Hispanic American Historical Review* 56 (August 1976): 438–60.

———. "Debt Servitude in Rural Guatemala, 1876–1936." *Hispanic American Historical Review* 63 (November 1983): 735–59.

———. "Development Aspects of the Construction of the Guatemalan Northern Railroad: The First Attempt, 1879–1885." Masters thesis, Tulane University Department of Latin American Studies, 1969.

———. "'This Life of Misery and Shame': Female Prostitution in Guatemala City, 1880–1920." *Journal of Latin American Studies* 18 (November 1986): 333–53.

Meade, Teresa, and Gregory Alonso Pirio. "In Search of the Afro-American 'Eldorado': Attempts by North American Blacks to Enter Brazil in the 1920s." *Luso-Brazilian Review* 25 (Summer 1988): 85–110.

Minority Rights Group, ed. *No Longer Invisible: Afro-Latin Americans Today.* London: Minority Rights Publications, 1995.

Montúfar, Rafael. *Caída de una tiranía: Páginas de la historia de Centro América (segunda parte).* Guatemala City: Sánchez & de Guise, 1923.

Moore, Alexander. "Symbolic Imperatives for Democratic Peace in Guatemala." In *Conflict, Migration, and the Expression of Ethnicity*, ed. Nancie L. González and Carolyn S. McCommon. Boulder, Colo.: Westview Press, 1989.

Mörner, Magnus, and Harold Sims. *Adventures and Proletarians: The Story of Migrants in Latin America*. Pittsburgh: University of Pittsburgh Press, 1977.

Mulzac, Hugh. *A Star to Steer*. New York: International Publishers, 1963.

Munro, Dana G. *The Five Republics of Central America: Their Political and Economic Development and Their Relations with the United States*. New York: Oxford University Press, 1918.

Nieman, Donald G., ed. *African Americans and The Emergence of Segregation, 1865–1900*. New York: Garland Publishing, 1994.

Obando Sánchez, Antonio. "Apuntes para la historia del movimiento obrero de Guatemala." *Alero* 30, tercera epoca (May–June 1978): 76–82.

———. *Memorias: La historia del movimiento obrero en Guatemala en este siglo*. Guatemala City: Editorial Universitaria, 1978.

Oliva Medina, Mario. *Artesanos y obreros costarricenses, 1880–1914*. San José: Editorial Costa Rica, 1985.

Opie, Frederick D. "Adios Jim Crow: Afro–North American Workers and the Guatemalan Railroad Workers' League, 1884–1921." Ph.D. diss., Syracuse University, 1999.

Painter, David S. Review of *The United States in Central America, 1860–1911: Episodes of Social Imperialism and Imperial Rivalry in the World System*, by Thomas Schoonover. In *Reviews in American History* 21 (June 1993): 267–71.

Palma Ramos, Danilo. "El negro en las relaciones etnicas de la segunda mitad del siglo XVIII y principios del siglo XIX en Guatemala." Tesis Licenciatura en Historia, Universidad de San Carlos de Guatemala Escuela de Historia, 1974.

Panama y la frutera: Análisis de una confrontación económico-fiscal. Panamá: Editorial Universitaria de Panamá, 1974.

Park, James William. *Latin American Underdevelopment*. Baton Rouge: Louisiana State University, 1995.

Parlee, Lorena M. "The Impact of the United States Railroad Unions on Organized Labor and Government Policy in Mexico, 1880–1911." *Hispanic American Historical Review* 64 (August 1984): 443–64.

Perman, Michael. *Struggle for Mastery: Disfranchisement in the South, 1888–1908*. Chapel Hill: University of North Carolina Press, 2001.

Petras, Elizabeth McLean. *Jamaican Labor Migration: White Capital and Black Labor, 1850–1930*. Boulder, Colo.: Westview Press, 1988.

Portes, Alejandro, and John Walton. *Labor, Class, and the International System*. New York: Academic Press, 1981.

Putnam, George Palmer. *The Southland of North America: Rambles and Observations in Central America during the Year 1912*. New York: G. P. Putnam's Sons, 1913.

Putnam, Lara. *The Company They Kept: Migrants and the Politics of Gender in Caribbean Costa Rica, 1870–1960*. Chapel Hill: University of North Carolina Press, 2002.

Quarles, Benjamin. *The Negro in the Making of America*. 2nd rev. ed. New York: Collier Books; London: Collier Macmillan, 1987.

Ramírez, Sergio, comp. and ed. *Sandino: The Testimony of a Nicaraguan Patriot, 1921–1934*. With an introduction and additional selections by Robert Edgar Conrad. Princeton, N.J.: Princeton University Press, 1990.

Reed, Merl E. "Lumberjacks and Longshoremen: The I.W.W. in Louisiana." *Labor History* 13 (Winter 1972): 41–62.

Reid, Ira De A. *The Negro Immigrant: His Background, Characteristics, and Social Adjustment, 1899–1937*. 1939, reprint: New York: AMS Press, 1970.

Rice, Lawrence D. *The Negro in Texas, 1874–1900*. Baton Rouge: Louisiana State University Press, 1971.

Rodney, Walter. *A History of the Guyanese Working People, 1881–1905*. Baltimore: Johns Hopkins University Press, 1981.

Rosenthal, Anton B. "Controlling the Line: Worker Strategies and Transport Capital on the Railroads of Ecuador, Zambia, and Zimbabwe, 1916–1950." Ph.D. diss., University of Minnesota, 1990.

Ross, Delmer G. "The Construction of the Railroads of Central America." Ph.D. diss., University of California at Santa Barbara, 1970.

———. *Development of Railroads in Guatemala and El Salvador, 1849–1929*. Lewiston, N.Y.: Edwin Mellen Press, 2001.

Rout, Leslie B., Jr. *The African Experience in Spanish America, 1502 to the Present Day*. London: Cambridge University Press, 1976.

Ruhl, Arthur Brown. *The Central Americans: Adventures and Impressions between Mexico and Panama*. New York: Charles Scribner's and Sons, 1928.

Sagastume, Rigoberto Urzua. "La empresa de los ferrocarriles de Guatemala como fuente de CESANTIA Laboral en el país: Análisis socio-político de la situación actual de los empleados indemnizados." Tesis Licenciatura, Universidad de San Carlos de Guatemala Facultad de Ciencias Jurídicas y Sociales, 1976.

Schell, William, Jr. *Integral Outsiders: The American Colony in Mexico City, 1876–1911*. Wilmington, Del.: SR Books, 2001.

Schlesinger, Stephen, and Stephen Kinzer. *Bitter Fruit: The Untold Story of the American Coup in Guatemala*. Garden City, N.Y.: Doubleday, 1982.

Schoonover, Thomas. *The United States in Central America, 1860–1911: Episodes of Social Imperialism and Imperial Rivalry in the World System*. Durham, N.C.: Duke University Press, 1991.

Scott, James C. *Domination and the Arts of Resistance: Hidden Transcripts*. New Haven, Conn.: Yale University Press, 1990.

Sernett, Milton C. *Bound for the Promised Land: African-American Religion and the Great Migration*. Durham, N.C.: Duke University Press, 1997.

Shugg, Roger W. "The New Orleans General Strike of 1892." *Louisiana Historical Quarterly* 21 (April 1938): 547–60.

———. *Origins of Class Struggle in Louisiana: A Social History of White Farmers and Laborers during Slavery and After, 1840–1875*. Louisiana: Louisiana State University Press, 1939.

Sims, Harold. *Adventures and Proletarians: The Story of Migrants in Latin America*. Pittsburgh: University of Pittsburgh Press, 1977.

Smith, Carol A., ed. *Guatemalan Indians and the State: 1540 to 1988*. Austin: University of Texas Press, 1990.

Spalding, Hobart A., Jr. *Organized Labor in Latin America: Historical Case Studies of Workers in Dependent Societies*. New York: New York University Press, 1977.

Spero, Sterling D., and Abram L. Harris. *The Black Worker: The Negro and the Labor Movement*. With a preface by Herbert G. Gutman. New York: Atheneum, 1968.

Stein, Judith. *The World of Marcus Garvey: Race and Class in Modern Society*. Baton Rouge: Louisiana State University Press, 1986.

Stewart, Watt. *Keith and Costa Rica: A Biographical Study of Minor Cooper Keith*. Albuquerque: University of New Mexico Press, 1964.

Suárez, Omar Jaén. *La población del istmo de Panamá del siglo XVI*. Panama City: N.p., 1979.

Sullivan-Gonzalez, Douglass. Review of *Doing Business with the Dictators: A Political History of United Fruit in Guatemala, 1899–1944*, by Paul J. Dosal. H-LatAm, H-Net Reviews, March 1996. http://www.h-net.org/reviews/showrev.php?id=342.

Takaki, Ronald. *Strangers from a Different Shore: A History of Asian Americans*. Boston: Little, Brown, 1989.

Thompson, Wallace. *Rainbow Countries of Central America*. New York: E. P. Dutton, 1926.

Thorton, John. *Africa and Africans in the Making of the Atlantic World, 1400–1680*. London: Cambridge University Press, 1992.

Torres-Rivas, Edelberto. *History and Society in Central America*. Translated by Douglass Sullivan-González. Austin: University of Texas Press, 1993.

Toussiant, Mónica. *Guatemala*. Textos de la historia de Centroamérica y el Caribe. Guadalajara: Instituto de Investigaciones "Dr. José María Luis Mora," Universidad de Guadalajara, Nueva Imagen, 1988.

Trefzger, Douglas W. "Immigration, Race, and Bananas: Toward a Social/Cultural History of Izabal, Guatemala." Conference paper presented at the LASA97 conference in Guadalajara, Mexico, April 17–19, 1997.

Vincent, Theodore G. "Black Hopes in Baja California: Black American and Mexican." *Western Journal of Black Studies* 21 (Fall 97): 204–14.

Vinicio Mejía, Marco. *Memorial del golfo dulce: Ecología política y enclaves en Guatemala*. Guatemala City: Editorial de La Real Academia, 1997.

Wade, Peter. *Blackness and Race Mixture: The Dynamics of Racial Identity in Colombia*. Baltimore: John Hopkins University Press, 1993.

Wagner, Regina. "Actividades empresariales de los alemanes en Guatemala, 1850–1920." *Mesoamérica* 13 (June 1987): 87–123.

Williams, John L. "The Rise of the Banana Industry and Its Influence on Caribbean Countries." M.A. thesis, Clark University, 1925.

Wilson, Charles Morrow. *Empire in Green and Gold: The Story of the American Banana Trade.* New York: Greenwood Press, 1968.

Winter, Nevin O. *Guatemala and Her People of Today.* Boston: L. C. Page & Co., 1909.

Woodward, C. Vann. *Origins of the New South, 1877–1913.* Baton Rouge: Louisiana State University Press, 1971.

———. *The Strange Career of Jim Crow.* New York: Oxford University Press, 1957.

Woodward, Ralph Lee, Jr. *Central America: A Nation Divided.* 2nd ed. Oxford: Oxford University Press, 1985.

———. "The Historiography of Modern Central America since 1960." *Hispanic American Historical Review* 67 (August 1987): 461–96.

———. *Rafael Carrera and the Emergence of the Republic of Guatemala, 1821–1871.* Athens: University of Georgia Press, 1993.

———. "The Rise and Decline of Liberalism in Central America: Historical Perspectives on the Contemporary Crisis." *Journal of Interamerican Studies and World Affairs* 26 (August 1984): 291–312.

Wright, Gavin. *Old South, New South: Revolutions in the Southern Economy since the Civil War.* New York: Basic Books, 1986.

Zimmerman, Marc. *Literature and Resistance in Guatemala: Textual Modes and Cultural Politics From El Señor Presidente to Rigoberta Menchú.* Vol. 1, *Theory, History, Fiction, and Poetry.* Monographs in International Studies, Latin American Series, no. 22. Athens: Ohio University Center for International Studies, 1995.

Index

Frederick Douglass Opie is Associate Professor of History and Director of the African Diaspora Program at Marist College. He is the author of *Hog and Hominy: Soul Food from Africa to America* (Columbia, 2008), *Black and Latino Relations in New York, 1959-2008* (Columbia, forthcoming), and he has published various articles.